TALKING DIRTY

See page 79

TALKING DIRTY

With an Introduction by
Jonathon Green

Cartoons by **Dan Pearce**

CASSELL

Cassell, an imprint of
Weidenfeld & Nicolson
Wellington House, 125 Strand, London, WC2R 0BB

First published in 2003

© Text copyright Jonathon Green 2003
© Cartoons copyright Dan Pearce

A CIP record for this book is available from the British Library

ISBN 0-304-36474-6

Distributed in the United States by Sterling Publishing Co. Inc.
387 Park Avenue South, New York, NY 10016–8810

Design by Gwyn Lewis

Printed in Great Britain by Clays Ltd, St Ives plc

CONTENTS

INTRODUCTION

Hello, hello? What have we here? Another *galère* of slang's grim-mest and most gut-wrenching. Gloriously illustrated by Mr Pearce in what I am delighted to categorize as the worst possible taste – but then the punishment ought to fit the crime and this latest selection of the ever-expanding database that is *Cassell's Dictionary of Slang* is nothing less, we must acknowledge, than reprehensible.

It is said by those who whinge about the 'decline' of language and – quite undeterred by fact – witter on like ancient mariners of 'consideration' or 'good manners", that speakers who turn to slang do so only through the paucity of their personal vocabulary. MEGO, as they are wont to say in God's Own Country: 'my eyes glaze over.' There are other phrases that might sum up such egregious silliness – many, many other phrases, and indeed you will find them in the pages that follow. But enough for now. The idea that slang corrals a dull, monotone, exclusively coarse subset of the mighty vocabulary that is English – whether of England, the US, Australia or any other Anglophone nation – would be no more than risible, were these naysayers less earnest in their foolishness. As it is, the slang lexicographer need but bend to his lexicon or hers (for the collection of this undoubtedly 'masculine' language – women use slang, but its point of view is almost overwhelmingly that of the XX chromosomes among us – is not exclusively male).

Here we do not find tedium, nor indeed a single tone. As to coarseness, how can one deny that it can of course be seen in a proportion of the slang vocabulary, but it is far from dominating. And if the language is coarse: should we, as the fearful and censorious prefer, murder the messenger in the hope of killing what he has to say? Humanity remains as nasty and brutish as ever, and if we are no longer quite so short, physical growth has in no way impeded our innate unpleasantness. So why should language be expected to collude in some Utopian fantasy? As Frank Zappa once adjured us: 'Do you love it, do you hate it? Here it is, the way you made it.' Never is this more true than in slang, which as I have opined before, is a 'counterlanguage', a form of words and speech which, quite consciously, sets itself against the standard English of the establishment and the orthodoxy.

The slang 'waterfront', as it were, is narrow but deep. Drink and drugs, sex, defecation, insults, money: these are the main preoccupations. A thin sliver of the Standard English vocabulary, and a serious lack of abstracts, but with slang's underlying desire to be not merely 'counter' but 'covert' too, it is endlessly reinventing itself. The first slang synonyms for 'drunk' were recorded around 1530; and they are still coming, around 2500 of them to date (while the Standard English word *drunk* is 650 years old and changes nary a phoneme). Similarly the terms for genitals (around 1000 per giblet), for fools (1800), for the world of drugs (4000) and so on. Size, as we piously intone, doesn't invariably matter – but slang does its best.

While slang's fecundity leans heavily towards single words or simple combinations, the slang dictionaries also yield a wondrous collection of phrases. And it is these phrases, some 5000 of them, that are assembled here. *Talking Dirty* is not a phrase book as such: its intention is amusement, and even edification; but not to render the user susceptible to an infinity of fights. This is not a volume wherein one enquires as to the problems of the postillion. A glance through the Contents should make things clear. Inevitably, it covers some of the ground explored by its three predecessors: here one will find filth, insults and bodily functions galore – now represented solely by phrasal expressions (a good number of which were excluded from the earlier volumes). But here also in abundance are acronymic and euphemistic phrases, phrases of affirmation, approbation, contempt, disbelief, dismissal, negation and outrage, plus a host of imprecations, oaths, toasts and threats – not to mention a myriad colourful expressions culled from the discourse of particular social groups, be they gays, Australians, the criminal underworld, the British upper classes or the African-American community in the United States. Use these phrases – all of them – if you will: but don't say you weren't warned.

Finally, a substantial tip of the hat to Ian Crofton, who transmuted the raw files into publishable and I trust amusing pages. As they say Down Under, 'yer blood's worth bottling'.

Jonathon Green

ABBREVIATIONS

abbr.	abbreviation, abbreviated
Anglo-Ind.	Anglo-Indian
Aus.	Australian
backsl.	backslang
Can.	Canadian
comb.	combination, combined
derog.	derogatory
dial.	dialect, dialectal
Du.	Dutch
esp.	especially
ety.	etymology
euph.	euphemism, euphemistic
excl.	exclamation
ext.	extended
fig.	figurative
Fr.	French
Ger.	German
Guyn.	Guyana, Guyanese

Ital.	Italian
joc.	jocular
juv.	juvenile
Lat.	Latin
lit.	literally
milit.	military
mispron.	mispronunciation
naut.	nautical
N.Z.	New Zealand
occas.	occasionally
orig.	originally
phr.	phrase
Port.	Portuguese
poss.	possible, possibly
pron.	pronounced
ref.	reference, referring
rhy. sl.	rhyming slang
RN	Royal Navy
Rus.	Russian
S. Afr.	South African
Scot.	Scottish
SE	Standard English
Sp.	Spanish
synon.	synonym, synonymous
sl.	slang
usu.	usually
W.I.	West Indies

HOW TO ENJOY *TALKING DIRTY*

Talking Dirty presents slang phrases under 94 category headings from Abuse to Worthless. The bulk of the categories are semantic/situational (e.g. being in a bad temper, breaking wind), but others are linguistic/tonal (e.g. acronymic phrases, euphemistic phrases) or group-related (e.g. phrases used by the gay community or by the criminal underworld). Each phrase is followed by a date in square brackets [18C], [19C], [late 18C–early 19C] and so on, indicating the period of usage of the phrase in question. The '+' sign indicates that a phrase is still in use, as does the date [2000s] which indicates a recent and current expression.

After the dates in square brackets comes a range of different types of information, including semantic or etymological glosses and usage labels indicating the geographical usage of the word e.g. (US) or the social/cultural usage, e.g. (US campus).

ABUSE, MISCELLANEOUS

See also DISBELIEF, SURPRISE, ANNOYANCE, EXCLAMATIONS
   THEREOF; DISMISSAL AND CONTEMPT, EXCLAMATIONS
   THEREOF; LEAVE ME ALONE; QUIET, PLEASE

bag your face! (also **go bag your head!**) [1980s+] (orig. US)

do as my shirt does! [18C–1940s] i.e. 'kiss my arse'

eat the big one [1980s+] (US)

fuck them all but six (and save them for pallbearers) [1910s+]
   (US, orig. milit.)

go soak your head! [late 19C+] (US)

go to hell and help your mother make bitch pie [mid-18C–
   late 19C]

lick me! [1970s+] (US campus)

m.f.u.t.u.! [1940s] (US) motherfuck you too!

Bag Your Face!

orchids to you! [1930s–1950s] (punning on *orchidectomy*, castration)

read my lips [1980s+] used to convey that one is thinking something insulting or obscene but choosing not to speak it (play on the use of the phrase in a campaign speech by ex-President George Bush in which he told the media, 'Read my lips, no more taxes')

screw you! [20C] (US)

shit in your hat! [20C]

shit in your teeth! [18C–mid-19C]

shit on you! [1930s+] (orig. US)

shove it up your nose! [1920s+] (orig. US)

sit on it and rotate! [1960s+] (US) suggesting that a hard and painful object be thrust into the subject's anus

stick it up your jumper! [1930s+] (usu. teen; transformed in Aus. to **stick it up your cunt!**)

suck eggs! [20C] (US)

take a carrot! [mid-19C] usu. to a woman

toss my salad [1990s+] (US prison) lick my ass

turd in your teeth! [17C]

up your clunge! [1990s] up your arse!

up your Ronson [1990s] i.e. up your *Ronson* lighter = shiter = anus

yank on that! [1980s+]

you are a mouth and you will die a lip [late 17C–mid-19C]

you are a thief and a murderer and you have killed a baboon and stolen his face [late 18C]

you're a waste of sperm/space/air [20C]

you're all about – like shit in a field [20C] you're a useful, alert, efficient person – like hell you are!

you're sorry as gully dirt [20C] (US) said to a worthless, contemptible person, or to one who fails to fit the local norms

May Ill Fortune Befall You

Some Australian imprecations:

may all the pores of your skin turn into little arseholes and cover you in shit

may the fleas of a thousand camels infest your armpits

Emus Kicking a Dunny Down

may the hairs up your arse turn into drumsticks and beat the
   shit out of you

may your arse cheeks turn into bicycle wheels and backpedal
   up your arse

may your chooks turn into emus and kick your dunny down
   (*chook* = chicken; *dunny* = outside lavatory)

may your ears turn into arseholes and shit on your shoulders

Smearing Another's Mother

another push and you'd have been a nigger [20C] the implication (in this context a slur) is that one's mother was happy to
   have sex with all races

go fuck your mother! [1930s+]

smell your mother! (also smell your monkey!) [1990s] usu.
   accompanied by waving the middle finger under the insultee's
   nose; the implication is of recent sexual foreplay

yo' mama! [1940s] (US Black) a general excl. which, like
   motherfucker, varies as to context, from the jovially
   teasing to the deliberately insulting; usu. used as a retort

your mother! [late 19C+] (orig. US, mainly teen) rejoinder
   to an insult, implying that whatever that insult is, it applies
   most to the speaker's own mother

Antipodean Barbs and Ripostes

get a woolly dog up ya = get lost

go and stick your head up a dead bear's bum

if I wanted to talk to an arsehole like you, I would 've farted!

I'll kick your bum till your nose bleeds!

Smelling a Monkey

I wish his dad had settled for a blow job

I wouldn't piss on you if you were on fire

last time I saw a mouth like that, it had a hook in it

pull your lip over your head and swallow!

she was so ugly that when she walked on the beach even the sewerage got up and left

stick your head up your Khyber Pass

what and your shit don't stink? said to someone who has a high opinion of himself

ya bloody wombat

you smell like a gorilla's armpit

you're a pain in the Gregory Peck = pain in the neck

you're as handy as shit on a stick = you're not much help

you're as ugly as a box of blowflies

you're fucked in the head and got shit for brains

you've got a face like a bashed-in shit can
you've got a head like a half-eaten pastie

Abusive Acronyms

a.k. [1920s–60s] (US) **1** an old fogey; from Yiddish *alter kocker* = old shit. **2** [1930s–70s] a toady; i.e. '*ass kisser*'

b.a. [20C] (W.I./Guyn) *big arse*

b.a.h. [20C] (US Black) a derog. description of a woman; i.e. '*bitch ass hoe*'

b.b. [20C] *bloody bastard*

b.o.b. [1990s] (US) an extremely obese woman; i.e. '*big old bitch*'

b.o.f. [1970s+] a tedious and conventional older person; i.e. '*boring old fart*'

b.p.n. [1900s–40s] a *bloody public nuisance*

c.a.b. [1990s] a general term of derision; i.e. '*complete arse bandit*'

d.a. [1970s] (US campus) *dumb ass*

d.ph. [1910s+] (US) *damned fool* (punning on *D.Phil.*)

f.b.i. [1990s] a general term of abuse, i.e. '*fucking bloody idiot!*'

f.o.b.b. [1970s] (US) a derog. description of a woman; i.e. '*fucked out boozy bitch*'

i.d.b. 1 [1920s+] *ignorant Dutch bastard.* **2** [1980s+] *in Daddy's business*

n.c.a.a. [1980s+] (US campus) a boorish person; i.e. '*no class at all*'

p.i.t.a. [1960s+] *pain in the ass*

s.a.b. [1980s+] (US campus) *social airhead bitch*

w.a.f.i. [1980s+] (Aus.) *wind-assisted fucking idiot*

w.a.f.i.

D.F.

ACRONYMS AND ABBREVIATIONS

See also ABUSE, MISCELLANEOUS; ADVISORY; CRIME AND THE
UNDERWORLD; DISMISSAL AND CONTEMPT, EXCLAMATIONS
THEREOF; DRUGS, DOING; DRUNK, GETTING AND BEING;
GAY; JOYS OF LIFE, THE; MENSTRUATION; MONEY; SARTORIAL
MATTERS; SEX, MOSTLY; SLIP

a.i.f. [1960s+] deaf (rhy. sl. *A.I.F.* = *A*ustralian *I*mperial *F*orces)

b.a. [1950s+] *b*ugger-*a*ll

b.a.b. [1980s+] (US) a nude bathing beach; i.e. '*b*are *a*ss *b*each'

b.d.t. [20C] (US) diarrhoea; i.e. '*b*ack-*d*oor *t*rots'

b.d.v. [1920s+] (tramp) a cigarette stub, picked up in the street;
i.e. '*b*end *d*own *V*irginia'

b.f.e./b.f.a. [1980s+] (US campus) somewhere very far away;
i.e. '*b*utt-*f*ucking *E*gypt', '*b*utt-*f*ucking *A*frica'

b.n. [1900s–30s] a *b*loody *n*uisance

c.r.s. [1980s+] (US campus) forgetful; i.e. '*c*an't *r*emember
*s*hit'

d.t.r. [1990s] (US campus) *d*efining *t*he *r*elationship; used of a
conversation, often between the partners

d.y.w.y.k. [late 19C] (US campus) a phr. of mocking dismissal
and exclusion; i.e. '*d*on't *y*ou *w*ish *y*ou *k*new'

f.f.v. [20C] (US) an important person or someone posing as
such; i.e. '*F*irst *F*amily of *V*irginia', a member of one of the
founding families of Virginia and thus one of the élite

f.h.b. [1910s+] used by a hostess when there is only enough to
feed the guests properly; i.e. '*f*amily *h*old *b*ack'

f.i.d.o. [1990s+] (US campus) a term of emotional resignation;
i.e. '*f*uck *i*t, *d*rive *o*n'

f.i.g.m.o. [1960s+] *fuck it*, *got my orders*; sometimes bowdlerized as 'finally I …' or 'forget it …'

f.i.l.t.h. [1980s+] used of someone who is attempting to resuscitate their career, stalled in London, in the Far East; i.e. '*failed in London, try Hong Kong*'

f.o.b. [1970s+] (N.Z.) a newly arrived coloured immigrant; i.e. '*fresh off the boat*'

f.t.b. [20C] *full to bursting*

f.t.d. [1910s] waste time on the job ('*fuck the dog*')

f.u.b.a.r. [1940s+] (orig. US milit.) **1** extremely unhappy. **2** totally beyond repair and/or control. **3** very drunk. **4** very unattractive. **5** doped out, exhausted; i.e. '*fucked up beyond all recognition*'

f.u.b.b. [1950s+] (orig. US milit.) in a parlous state; i.e. '*fucked up beyond belief*'

f.y.f.i. [1990s] appended to memos in business; i.e. '*for your fucking information*'

g.o.m.e.r. [1960s+] (US) an old, dirty, difficult or chronically ill hospital patient; i.e. '*get out of my emergency room*'

g.o.r.k. [1960s+] (US campus) an inadequate, an incompetent; i.e. '*God only really knows*'

g.t.f.o.o.m.w. [1990s] *get the fuck out of my way*

j.a.p. [1970s+] (US) a rich, spoiled Jewish girl; i.e. '*Jewish-American princess*'

j.f.d.i. [1990s+] *just fucking do it*

l.u.g. [1980s+] (US campus) a female student who is not necessarily lesbian, but who identifies with feminism and lesbian politics and culture; i.e. '*Lesbian Until Graduation*'

m.a.f. [1990s] extremely annoyed; i.e. '*m*ad *a*s *f*uck'

m.r.a. [1980s+] (US campus) unsociable behaviour; i.e. '*m*ajor *r*eeb *a*ction' (*reeb*, socially inept person)

n.b.d. [1980s+] (US campus) a general expression of nonchalance; i.e. '*n*o *b*ig *d*eal'

n.b.g. [20C] *n*o *b*loody *g*ood

n.f.g. [1970s+] (US) *n*o *f*ucking *g*ood

n.f.w. [1970s+] (US) *n*o *f*ucking *w*ay!

n.m.c. [1990s+] (UK juv.) a metaphorical 'club' whose members are the least popular children at school; i.e. '*n*o *m*ates *c*lub'

n.s.s. [1980s+] (US campus) a retort to a stupid question or statement; '*n*o *s*hit, *S*herlock' (the 'Sherlock' being the fictional detective Sherlock Holmes)

o.m.d. [late 19C] (US) a pretty, but empty-headed girl; i.e. '*o*ld *m*en's *d*arlings'

o.p.t. [20C] *o*ther *p*eople's *t*obacco; always popular among poverty-stricken smokers

o.t.d. [1980s+] (US) gone, departed; i.e. '*o*ut *t*he *d*oor'

o.t.l. [1950s-70s] (US campus) not in touch with reality, inattentive, unaware; i.e. '*o*ut *t*o *l*unch'

p.d.q. [late 19C] *p*retty *d*amn *q*uick

poet's day [1970s+] Friday; i.e. '*p*iss *o*ff *e*arly, *t*omorrow's *S*aturday'

s.a.b.u. [1940s] *s*elf-adjusting *a*rmy *b*alls-*u*p

s.b.d. [1960s+] a silent, foul-smelling fart; i.e. '*s*ilent *b*ut *d*eadly'

s.e.g.

s.e.g. [1980s] (US campus) a toadying or hypocritical smile;
i.e. 'shit-eating grin'

s.f.a. [1940s+] nothing; i.e. 'sweet fuck all', 'sweet Fanny
Adams'

s.n.a.f.u. [1940s+] messed up, gone wrong; i.e. 'situation
normal, all fucked/fouled/frigged up'

s.o.l. [1930s+] (Aus.) a bad temper; i.e. 'shit on one's liver'

s.o.s. [1940s+] (US) the same thing as usual; i.e. 'same old shit'

The African-American Acronym

b.m.t. [1990s] a phr. designed to affirm one's authority, masculinity, etc. and thus reinforce one's argument; i.e. 'Black man talking'

B.N.I.C./H.N.I.C. [1930s+] a sarcastic reference to any Black authority-figure; i.e. 'Black Nigger in charge'; 'Head Nigger in charge'

d.a.n. [2000s] a fool; i.e. 'dumb-ass nigger'

g.s.p. [1990s] anyone who treats one badly or contemptuously; golden shower people, i.e. those who (in slang) 'piss on you'

k.i.m.b.a. [1990s+] (teen) kiss my Black ass

o.p.b. [1930s–50s] a hypothetical brand of cigarettes; used by one who rarely purchases their own; i.e. 'other people's brand'

o.p.p. [1990s] **1** other people's property, usu. their wife, husband or partner. **2** other people's pussy; i.e. the wives and girlfriends of other men

p.h.a.t. [1960s+] from physically attractive; or pretty hips and thighs; or pretty hips, ass, tits; or pretty hot and tempting; or pussy, hips, ass and thighs

t.c.b. 1 [1950s+] to deal with matters in hand; take care of business. **2** [2000s] behaviour seen as stereotypically White, i.e. 'typical cracka behaviour'

w.h.i.p.s. [1960s+] the White establishment and/or the police; i.e. 'white power structure'

t.f.a. [1980s+] (US campus) wonderful, exceptional, very good; i.e. '*t*oo *f*ucking *a*wesome'

t.g.i.f. [mid-20C+] *t*hank *G*od *i*t's *F*riday

t.k.o. [1950s+] (orig. US) to defeat in theory if not in practice (from boxing jargon, '*t*echnical *k*nock-*o*ut')

t.s. [1940s+] (orig. US milit.) *t*ough *s*hit (often used ironically or mockingly as well as sympathetically)

t.s.h. [1980s+] (US campus) expression of commiseration; i.e. '*t*hat *s*hit *h*appens'

u.m.s. [1980s+] (US campus) a sudden, unpredictable change of mood; i.e. '*u*gly *m*ood *s*wing'

Four Politically Incorrect Acronyms

A.P.T. [1920s–1960s] unpunctuality; i.e. '*A*frican *p*eople's *t*ime' (the offensive stereotype is that Blacks have a less immediate sense of time than their White peers)

B.M.T. [1990s] unpunctuality; i.e. '*B*lack *m*an's *t*ime'

C.P.T. [20C] an hour or two later than the prescribed time; i.e. '*c*oloured *p*eople's *t*ime'

J.S.T. [1960s+] (US) *J*ewish *S*tandard *T*ime, i.e. not punctual.

The Secret Language of the Upper Classes

a.d. [late 19C–1900s] *a d*rink; used on dance cards to disguise a preference for *a*lcohol over *d*ancing

b.y.t. [1940s] *b*right *y*oung *t*hings

D.I.O. [late 18C–mid-19C] *d*amme! *I*'m *o*ff; the phr. satirizes the various forms of polite initials left on visiting cards at the time

m.t.f. [1980s+] an overly amorous young man; i.c. '*m*ust *t*ouch *f*lesh'

n.b. [1980s+] *n*o *b*ackground

n.d. [late 19C] a woman who is attempting to appear younger than she is; from the bibliographical annotation *n.d.* = *n*o *d*ate

n.n. [late 19C] a husband; i.e. '*n*ecessary *n*uisance'

p.p.c. [late 19C] a curt, barely polite farewell; from Fr. *p*our *p*rendre *c*ongé = to take leave (written on a visiting card)

p.p.m. [late 19C] goodbye, as inscribed on visiting cards; from Fr. *p*our *p*'tit *m*oment = for a little while

s.o.h.f. [1970s+] *s*ense *o*f *h*umour *f*ailure; often discerned in someone who fails to appreciate the throwing of bread rolls, baiting of minorities, etc.

t.b. [1980s] (UK teen) *trè*s *b*rill, absolutely wonderful; from Fr. *trè*s, very + *b*rill

t.b.a. [20C] (US) a young man who is *t*o *b*e *a*voided

w.h.b. [late 19C–1900s] men who take unwanted liberties with women; i.e. '*w*andering *h*and *b*rigade'

ADVISORY

Carpe Diem

don't let your meat loaf [1960s+] (US) a general phr. of encouragement, the implication being 'don't procrastinate'

shit or get off the pot! [1940's+] make a decision – or let someone else do it for you!

you can't take it with you [mid-19C+] a phr. urging someone to spend their money, enjoy their possessions etc.

you gotta let yer nutz hang [1990s] (US Black teen) be yourself, don't let anybody dictate to you

you'll be a long time dead [late 19C+] a phr. addressed to anyone the speaker feels is wasting time, not putting their life to its best advantage etc.

Don't Let Your Meat Loaf

Pray Keep Calm and Fret Not

don't get your bowels in an uproar [20C]

don't get your breeches torn [1960s] (US)

don't get your shit hot [20C]

don't let your (alligator) mouth overload your ass [1960s+] (US) keep quiet, esp. in a difficult situation where words might complicate matters

don't lose your hair [late 19C]

don't strip your gears [1940s–60s] (orig. US Black)

don't worry – it may never happen [1910s+] usu. offered as advice to someone looking especially miserable or worried

gently, Bentley [1940s–60s] (a catchphrase used by Jimmy Edwards in BBC Radio's *Take It From Here* (1940–60))

you can't fly on one wing [1940s+] (Can.) have another drink before you go

---

Advisory Acronyms

c.y.a. [1950s+] (orig. US milit.) look after yourself before worrying about anyone else, be it colleagues, customers, or the wider world; i.e. '*cover your ass*'

k.b.o. [1940s] *keep buggering on*

k.i.s.s. [1960s+] (US) *keep it simple, stupid*

t.i.l.i.s [1990s] (US Black) be absolutely candid, hold nothing back; i.e. '*tell it like it is*'

Illegitimis non carborundum/nil carborundum illegitimi [1940s+] (orig. milit.) don't let the bastards grind you down (the 'Latin' is hardly accurate)

don't all speak at once [late 19C+] used when one has called for volunteers (for something unpleasant or unappealing) and no one has spoken up

if it moves, salute it; if it don't, paint it [1940s+] (orig. milit.) supposedly the advice for a successful (services) career

Probity

don't let your mouth write a check your ass can't cash [1960s+] (orig. US Black) keep quiet, esp. when speaking might make matters worse

don't spend it all at once [1960s+] joc. advice usu. offered on handing over a very small amount of money, in payment of a debt etc.

don't take any wooden money/rubber nickels [1920s] beware of being defrauded or hoaxed

keep your hand on your ha'penny till the right man turns up [1900s–20s] advice to young women to retain their virginity until the advent of 'Mr Right'

Shedding Illusions and Thereby Getting Real

don't give up the day job [1990s+] joc. and deflatory suggestion to one who has announced their latest (usu. implausible/
fantastic) idea for self-improvement

don't hang dirty washing in my backyard [1940s] (US Black)
don't lie to me; don't tell me stories

don't hold your breath [1960s+] (orig. US) phr. used of an
unreliable person or of a promise that may not be kept; i.e.
don't expect anything to happen, don't expect promises to
materialize

don't make me laugh [1920s+] don't be stupid, ridiculous; thus
[1920s–40s] ext. as **don't make me laugh I've got a split lip**

don't sell me a dog [late 19C] (UK society) don't try to fool me
(ref. to the perceived lack of ethics in such a transaction)

Farting Against Thunder

don't do anything I wouldn't do [20C] exhortation to anyone who is leaving, esp. on holiday or in search of similar supposed pleasures; the implication is usu. sexual, and the point is to wish them as excessive a time as possible

don't do anything you couldn't eat [1930s+] (Aus.) similar to the above

---

you can't shit a shitter (also **don't bullshit a bullshitter**) [1950s+] you can't fool someone who deals in fooling others

you can't fart against thunder [late 19C+] don't attempt the impossible

you can't fight city hall [20C] (US) you can't win against the establishment

AFFIRMATION

absofuckinglutely [1910s+]

all the way down [mid-19C–1910s]

boots and all [1940s+] (Aus./N.Z.)

both ways from the ace (also **both ways from the jack**) [1910s] (US)

by the clock [1920s] (US)

damn-but [1930s–40s] (Irish)

dead on [late 19C]

for real! [1950s+]

fucking A! [1950s+]

hole in one! [1970s+]

honest-to-God! (also **honest-to-goodness, honest-to-gosh**) [1910s+]

honest to John! (also **honest to Pete**) [1950s+] (US)

hot ticket! [1960s+] (US campus)

I guess yes! [late 19C] (US)

I'll say! [1920s+] (orig. US)

indeed and indeed [late 17C–mid-19C]

naked! [1970s+] (US campus)

whatever floats your boat [1980s+] (US campus) an expression of acceptance, I agree, you're right

you ain't just whistling Dixie! [20C] (US)

you bet! (also **you betcha!, you betcher!**) [mid-19C+] (orig. US)

you better believe it (also **you better know it, don't you believe it!**) [mid-19C+]

you can kiss the Book on that! [late 19C]

you can put a ring round that one [1920s+] (N.Z.)

you're darn tootin' (also **you're durn tootin', you're damn tootin'**) [20C] (orig. US)

you're telling me [1930s]

A Bear Shitting in the Woods

The Brothers are in Agreement
with the Proposition

… and indicate their assent as follows:

ain't it! [1940s–60s] (US Black)

damn straight! [1970s+] (orig. US Black)

give it a name! (also **name it!**) [1930s–50s] (US Black)

I feel you! [1960s+] (US Black)

straight ahead! [1960s] (US Black)

tell the truth! [1950s+] (US Black)

Thank You for Stating the Bleedin' Obvious …

are the Kennedys gun-shy?

can a duck swim?

can niggers dance?

do bears shit in the woods?

do beavers piss on flat rocks?

does a koala shit in a gum tree and wipe his arse on a cockatoo?

Sure as …

- a gun [20C]
- God made little green apples [20C] (US)
- shit [1970s+]
- you're a foot high [late 19C–1950s] (US)
- I'm a man fit to wear britches [19C]

A Koala Wiping his Arse on a Cockatoo

does a teddy bear have cotton balls?

does Superman fly in his underwear?

do fish swim?

is cock-sucking fun?

is pig pussy pork?

is the Pope Catholic?

they got cows in Texas?

would a cat eat liver?

ANNOY, TO

See also BAD TEMPER, BEING IN OR GETTING INTO A;
   DISBELIEF, SURPRISE, ANNOYANCE

break someone's melt (or **knock in someone's melt**) [20C]
   (Ulster)

muck around [late 19C+]

stick in someone's throat (also **stick in someone's crop**,
   stick in someone's neck) [20C]

to get …

– funny with [late 19C+]

   someone's goat (also **get on someone's goat**) [20C]

– on someone's tit [1980s] (US campus)

– on someone's back [1950s+]

– on someone's jock [1980s+] (US Black)

– under someone's skin (orig. US) [20C]

– up someone's arse/ass/hole/butt [1970s+] (US) immediately
   behind and so irritating

– **up someone's back** [1980s+] (US)

wouldn't that jar you? [late 19C–1930s] (US) wouldn't that infuriate you?

If so, the one infuriated may say:

back up off my tip [2000s] (US Black teen) don't annoy me

ANXIOUS *See* NERVOUS, ANXIOUS, AGITATED

A.S.A.F.P. (AT ONCE, IF YOU PLEASE)

a.s.a.f.p. [1980s+] (US campus) i.e. '*as soon as fucking possible*', derived from the standard business expression *a.s.a.p.*

at the drop of a hat (also **at the drop of the flag**) [mid-19C+] (orig. US)

before one can say Jack Robinson [19C]

in a brace of shakes (also **in a couple of shakes**) [early 19C+]

in a flea's leap [mid-19C]

in a pig's whisper [19C]

in a shake (of a hand) [early 19C]

in half a shake [1930s+]

in less than no time [mid-19C+]

in the blowing of a match [late 19C]

in two twos [mid-19C+]

like a blink (also **like blinko**) [1900s–30s]

like a shot [early 19C+]

no sooner calved than licked [20C] (Irish) dealt with immediately

off the hooks [mid-19C]

off the top [1990s+] (US)

one-two-three [20C]

on the knocker [1930s+] (Aus.) on demand, esp. of cash payments

on the nail [late 16C+] exactly, immediately, as required (usu. as regards payments)

right off the bat (also **hot off the bat**) [20C] (orig. US)

right off the reel (also **off the reel**, **right off the rail**) [late 19C+] (US)

AVE ATQUE VALE: 'HAIL AND FAREWELL'

Greetings

bhani ghani! (also **behani ghani!**) [1960s–70s] (US Black) a greeting favoured by supporters of Black Power (poss. from Swahili *abari gani*, what's news?)

come in Berlin [1970s] (US campus)

Did They Forget to Feed the Dingoes?

did they forget to feed the dingoes? [1960s+] (Aus.) used
to greet an unexpected arrival

getting much? [1920s+] (US) a male-to-male greeting

give me five! (also **slip me five!**) [1910s+] (orig. US
Black) a greeting usu. accompanied by ritual palm
slapping

give the drummer some [1950s+] (US Black) as above

hi-de-hi ... ho-de-ho [1940s+] popular style of greeting and
the requisite response (orig. used by the US bandleader Cab

Calloway in 'The Hi-De-Ho Man', but popularized in the BBC TV sitcom *Hi De Hi!* (1970s–80s), which was set in a 1950s holiday camp)

how (are) they hanging? [1950s+] a man-to-man greeting

howdy doody! [late 19C+] (US)

how's your box? [20C] (US Black)

how's it bouncing? [20C] (US)

how's she cutting? [1980s+] (Irish)

how's your ass? [1960s+] (US)

how you making it? [mid-19C+] (prison)

like hi [1990s+] (US campus)

lay some on me! [1950s+] (US Black) an invitation to swap ritual hand slaps

let's talk trash [1920s+] (US Black)

look what the wind's blown in [1920s+]

olly, olly! [20C] (Cockney) i.e. hello, hello!

que pasa? [1980s+] (US campus) (Sp. 'what's happening?')

How Are You ...

- **blowing?** [1920s] (Irish)
- **diddling?** [1970s]
- **hitting them?** [late 19C+] (US)
- **off for soap?** [mid–late 19C]
- **popping (up)?** [late 19C–1940s] (Aus.)

---

shake five! [1950s+] (W.I.) a greeting between two men

skin me! [1950s+] (US Black) a form of greeting involving ritual palm slapping

stud horse! [mid-19C+] (US) a greeting between men

's up [1980s+] (US Black/campus/teen)

what does it look like? [1970s] (US campus)

what do you know? [1910s+]

what it B like? [1980s+] (US Black gang) greeting used by the Bloods, one of the two leading Los Angeles gangs; their rivals, the Crips, use **what it C like?**

what's jumping? [1980s+] (US campus)

what's krackalackin? [20C] (US Black)

what's on the agenda, Brenda? [20C] (US)

what's the story, morning glory? [1940s+] (orig. US Black)

what's the word? Thunderbird! [1950s–60s] (US Black) greeting based on a ref. to *Thunderbird*, a sweet fortified wine

what's tickin', chicken? [20C] (US)

what up dog? [1990s] (US Black teen)

yaga-yaga! [1980s+] (W.I./UK Black teen)

Adieux

Abyssinia! [1930s+] (orig. US)

adios amoebas [1980s] (US campus)

a.m.f. [1960s+] a euph. abbr., goodbye, that's it, it's all over; i.e. '*a*dios, *m*otherfucker', euph. as '*a*dios, *m*y *f*riend'

au reservoir! (also **over the reservoir**) [mid-19C–1920s] (orig. US) (from Fr. *au revoir*, goodbye)

A Hasty Banana

be lucky [1930s+] (mainly London)

bung ho! [1920s+]

catch you (later) [1970s+] (orig. US Black)

catch you on the flip flop/side [1970s] (US campus)

check you (later) [1980s+] (orig. US Black)

chow for now [1990s] (US campus) from Ital. *ciao* (pron. 'chow'), goodbye

dig you later [1940s+]

e ya later [1990s+] (US teen)

g.b. [1970s] (US campus) i.e. '*goodbye*'

get back [1980s+] (US campus)

go easy [1990s+] (US teen)

hasta la pasta! [1990s+] (US campus) (from Sp. *hasta la vista*, see you later)

hasty banana! [1940s+] (US)

hooray fuck! [1950s+] (N.Z.) used as a farewell to someone one dislikes or has just been insulting

I'm archives [1980s+] (US campus)

I'm in the wind [20C] (orig. US prison)

I'm out of here [1970s+]

it's been real [1970s+] (orig. US campus) (also used ironically)

keep it between the ditches (US) ('it' being a metaphorical vehicle)

kiss kiss [1990s] (US campus)

later, tater [1970s] (US campus)

little more! [1950s+] (W.I. Rasta)

mawgabraw! [20C] (Irish) usu. delivered as a parting shot, i.e. 'go to hell!'

my feet are staying [1980s+] (US campus)

olive oil [late 19C–1970s] (orig. music-hall) (mispron. of Fr. *au revoir*, goodbye)

osmosis amoebas! [1980s+] (US campus)

Paul Revere [1980s+] (US campus) (play on Fr. *au revoir*, goodbye, and the US Revolutionary hero)

peace out! (also **peace up!**) [1990s] (US campus/teen)

... In a While, Crocodile!

pip pip! [late 19C] (from a street cry launched at passing cyclists in the late 19C, when bicycles were still a novelty)

plant you now, dig you later [1930s–60s] (US Black)

smell you (also **smell you later**) [1990s] (US campus)

stay loose! [1970s+] (esp. in communities influenced by California's post-hippie era 'new therapies')

stick with it! [1960s+]

take it easy, greasy [1930s–40s] (US Black)

teuf-teuf [1900s–20s]

tiddly-push [1920s–30s]

tinkerty-tonk [1920s–30s]

toodle-pip [1920s–30s]

t.t.f.n. [1940s+] i.e. '*ta-ta* for *now*' (orig. coined in Tommy Handley's BBC radio show, *ITMA* (1939–49) and long associated with BBC disc jockey Jimmy Young)

you're so tan I hate you [1990s] (US campus)

See You ...

- **anonski** [1930s–50s] (orig. Aus.)

- **in court** [1960s+]

- **in the funny papers** [1920s+] (US)

- **in the soup** [20C] (Aus.)

- **later, alligator … in a while, crocodile** [1950s–60s] (popularized by the 1956 Bill Haley and the Comets pop hit of the same name (written by R.C. Guidry): 'See you lat-er, al-li-ga-tor,/Aft-er 'while, croc-o-dile,/Can't you see you're in my way, now,/Don't you know you cramp my style?', and by the widely publicized use of the phr. by Princess Margaret (1930–2002))

BAD TEMPER, BEING IN OR GETTING INTO A

See also ANNOY, TO

Chucking a Mental: The Abandonment of Sang-Froid

blow one's cork [1930s+]

blow one's roof [1950s] (US)

blow one's stack [1940s+]

boil over [mid–late 19C]

bug out [1970s+]

bung/stack on an act [1920s+] (Aus.) to lose one's temper and deliver a stream of obscenities

burst a blood-vessel [20C]

burst one's boiler [early–mid-19C]

catch on fire [late 19C]

chew the carpet [1950s+] (US)

chew the rug [late 19C+] (US)

chuck a mental [1980s+] (Aus.)

chuck a mickey [1950s+] (Aus.)

chuck a sixer [1940s+] (Aus.) (from *sixer*, a scoring kick in Australian rules football)

chuck a spas [1990s] (Aus.) (from SE *spastic*, a person suffering from spastic paralysis)

climb the rigging [1910s+]

do a loony [1990s+] (UK juv.)

do the lolly [1940s+] (Aus.)

drop plates (on this mother) [1970s] (US Black) to get sufficiently annoyed to resort to physical violence

flare up [mid-19C+]

flip one's top [1940s–50s] (US Black)

flip one's wig [1930s+]

fly hot [1900s–30s] (US Black)

fly off (the handle) [19C+] (orig. US)

fly the coop [mid-19C+]

fly to flinders [20C] (US) (from SE *flinders*, fragments, splinters)

fly up in the air [19C+] (US)

get ignorant [20C] (W.I.)

get in one's rickaticks [20C] (W.I.)

get into a paddy [late 19C+]

get off one's bike [1930s+] (Aus./N.Z.)

Chewing the Carpet

get one's hair off [19C+]

get on/stand on one's hind legs [late 19C+]

get out of one's pram [1950s+]

get out one's mad [1920s+] (Aus.)

get the ass [1970s+] (US Black/campus)

get the mohawk [1950s+] (US teen) build up one's irritation

– **fruit** [1970s]

– **melon** [20C]

– **nana** [1940s+]

– **nut** [1910s+]

– **scone** [1940s+] (Aus./N.Z.)

– **top** [1910s+]

into a genuine bad temper (from stereotyping of Native Americans as unpredictably violent)

get the pricker [1940s–60s] (Aus./N.Z.)

get the shits [20C] (Aus.)

get (up) on one's ear [19C+] (US)

get wet [late 19C–1940s] (Aus.)

grow horns [1970s+] (US campus)

hit the ceiling [1910s+]

knap the rust [19C]

lead off [1910s+] (orig. milit.)

nut up [1970s+]

poke one's mouth off [1970s+] (US Black)

pop a tuck [1970s]

pop one's cork [1960s+]

rain on (someone) [1920s+]

shoot off (at the mouth) [mid-19C+]

spill one's guts [1920s+]

spit one's guts [1930s]

spit out the dummy [1980s] (Aus.)

suffer a u.m.s., [1980s+] (US campus) i.e. '*u*gly *m*ood *s*wing'

take the huff [mid-19C+]

take the needle [20C] (Irish)

throw a benny [1990s+] (juv.)

throw a six [1940s+] (Aus.) (poss. from craps dice, or a play on *sick*)

Getting One's Thingmy Up

Namely, **getting one's ...**

– **African up** [20C] (US)

– **dander up** [19C+] (orig. US)

– **dandruff up** [20C] (US)

– **hackles up** [19C+]

– **Indian up** [late 19C+]

– **Irish up** [19C+]

– **monkey up** [early–mid-19C+]

– **nigger up** [20C] (US)

– **tail-feathers up** [20C] (US)

Places or Conditions Arrived at or Entered into when One Embarks upon a Wobbly

In such circumstances, **one goes …**

– **ballistic** [1980s+]
– **butcher's hook** [1940s+] (Aus.)
– **crook** [1910s+]
– **into one** [1990s+]
– **into orbit** [1960s+]
– **lemony (at someone)** [1940s–50s] (Aus./ N.Z.)
– **off at the lip** [20C] (Can./US)
– **postal** [1990s+] (US teen)
– **spare** [1940s]
– **through the roof** [1950s+]
– **to market** [late 19C+]
– **to the moon** [1930s] (Ulster)
– **up in the air** [19C+]
– **up the wall** [1950s+]

Lose One's …

– **cool** [1950s+] (orig. US)
– **hair** [1930s]
– **rag** [1950s+]
– **vest** [19C]
– **wool** [early 19C–1940s]

Going into Orbit

Mad as ...

– **a buck** [late 16C–early 17C]

– **a meat axe** [1920s+]

– **a wet hen** [early 19C+]

– **hops** [mid-19C+] (US)

Not only that, but ...

madder than a cow's tit on a cold day [1970s] (US)

In a Duck Fit: Being Ever So Cross

all hair by the nose [20C] (US)

at the house-roof [16C]

at the top of the house [mid-17C–mid-19C]

bent out of shape [mid-19C+] (US)

brassed off [1940s+]

browned off [1930s+] (orig. milit.) (from the accumulation of rust on old or neglected metal; also poss. a ref. to sodomy)

cross as two sticks [mid-19C–1920s]

have a case of the ass [1960s+] (US campus)

have a farting spell [20C]

have one's jaws tight [1960s–70s] (US Black)

having got out of bed on the wrong side [early 19C+]

hot as a (three-dollar) pistol [20C]

hot enough to fuck [1960s+] (US)

in a duck fit [1900s–20s] (US)

in a fling [mid-19C–1900s]

in Crab Street [early 19C] (from *crab*, to upset, annoy)

like a cock-maggot in a sink-hole [late 19C–1920s]

off one's block [1920s+]

off one's rag [1990s+] (UK juv.)

off the hook [20C] (US)

on someone's ear [mid-19C+] (US)

on the cross-cut (with someone) [1900s] (N.Z.)

on the gee [1920s] (i.e. *gee*d up)

on the pot [mid-19C]

on the prod/peck [20C] (US)

out for a pelter [late 19C–1900s] (dial. *pelter*, bad temper)

pissed off [1940s+] (orig. US)

simply throwing up buckets [late 19C–1900s] (Aus.)

sore as a boil/boiled owl/gum boil [20C] (orig. Aus.)

sore as a snouted sheila [1940s+] (Aus.) cross as a woman
who has been 'stood up'

up a tree [1970s+] (US campus)

up in the air [19C+]

up in the boughs [17C+]

BORING (CRASHINGLY)

dull as dog shit [1970s+]

fair crow [20C] (Aus./N.Z.) something inexpressibly tedious or baffling (the crow being a bird of traditionally bad omen)

grape on the business [1940s+] a bore, one who depresses or irritates the company by their presence (?from sour *grapes*)

he is too much with us [late 19C] (UK society) said of a bore

he reminds me of a stunned mullet [1950s+] (Aus.)

Awkward Social Situations No. 1

What to Say to an Entirely Boring Person

beam me up, Scotty, there's no intelligent life here [1970s] (US campus) (coined in the *Star Trek* TV series)

di-da, di-da, di-da [1930s+]

fuck that noise! [1980s+] (US)

haste it up! [1940s] (Aus.)

I don't like this movie [1960s+] (US)

if your aunt had balls, she'd be your uncle [20C] used as a rejoinder to a speaker who has just finished a long and laborious explanation of the obvious

is that a stick up your arse? [1960s+]

next topic, please [1990s+] (US teen)

one of these fine days you'll wake up and find yourself dead [20C]

you could talk under water/wet cement [1970s+] (Aus.)

A Stunned Mullet

it's going to rain [1950s–60s] a phr. used to indicate boredom,
  e.g. *I think it's going to rain*, indicating that it is time to leave
  a dull gathering or party

let's lose Charley [1950s–60s] a term used among intimates
  who want to get rid of a bore in their company

make one tired [late 19C+] (orig. US) to bore

she's total anguish [1940s–50s] (UK middle class) she is
  unutterably tedious

Pas de Tich!

no Tich! [mid-19C] (UK society) don't be dull, that's boring (ref. to the near-inevitability, at a certain era, of dinner-table conversations centring on the *Tichborne Claimant* case, in which Arthur Orton (1834–98) claimed in 1866 to be Roger Charles Tichborne (1829–54), the heir to an English baronetcy, who was lost at sea. Orton was finally discredited and imprisoned in 1874)

pas de Lafarge [mid-19C] (UK society) a similar expression (referring to the French case of the alleged poisoner Madame *Lafarge*)

BRAGGADOCIO

Bragging, vain empty boasting (from the name of a vainglorious character in Spenser's Faerie Queene*)*

See also BRAVERY; COWARDS AND WEAKLINGS

full of himself [late 19C+]

he's got an alligator mouth and a hummingbird/canary ass [1960s+] (US) he brags but has insufficient courage to back up his words

he straps it to his ankle [1970s+] said of a sexual braggart (his penis is so large he has to 'strap it to his ankle')

high in the instep [mid-16C–late 18C]

high in tooth [late 19C]

high on himself [1930s+] (US)

la-di-dah (also **laa-dee-laa**) [mid-19C+]

his trumpeter is dead [late 18C–early 19C] said of a braggart, a self-advertiser (he has to sound his own trumpet)

on one's high horse [late 18C+]

shit weighs heavy [late 19C+] (Can.) a phr. used of a braggart

six feet above contradiction [late 19C] (US) absolutely certain, totally arrogant, impervious to any argument

up himself [1940s+] (Aus.)

uppity-ass [mid-19C+] (orig. US)

you couldn't hit him/her in the behind with a red apple [1990s] (US Black) used of a conceited or arrogant person

All Mouth and No Trousers

all gab and guts (like a young crow) [20C] (Ulster)

all mouth and no trousers (also **all mouth, all mouth and trousers**) [late 19C+]

all piss /piddle and wind like the barber's dog /cat [1940s+] (Aus./N.Z.)

all prick and breeches [1920s+]

all pricks and no pence [20C]

all wind and piss [late 19C+]

BRAVERY AND GENERAL SOUNDNESS

See also BRAGGADOCIO; COWARDS AND WEAKLINGS

all oak and iron bound [19C+] dependable (the ref. is to the Royal Navy's 'wooden walls', its men o' war)

all wool and a yard wide (also **all wool and no shoddy**) [late 19C+] excellent, dependable (from *shoddy*, material made from wool waste)

game as a meat ant (also **game as an ant**) [1930s+] (Aus.) very brave

game as a pissant [late 19C+] (Aus.) brave, courageous

have sand in one's craw/in one's gizzard [19C] (US) to be brave

game as a pebble (also **game as pebbles**) [mid-19C+] extremely courageous, 'raring to go'.

game as Ned Kelly [1930s+] (Aus.) plucky, courageous, willing to go up against overwhelming odds

mettle to the back [late 16C–mid-18C] very brave, utterly dependable

more guts than a Bedford truck [1990s] (Aus.) used of a brave and admirable individual

on a brave [mid–late 19C] (US) suddenly and temporarily courageous

one hundred per cent (also **a hundred per cent**) [20C] dependable, loyal

BREAKFASTING

Miscellaneous Breakfasts

cowboy's breakfast [1950s] (mainly juv.) baked beans

hell for breakfast (also **hellbent for breakfast**) [20C] rushed, hurriedly, at top speed

nine ways from breakfast [1970s+] in all sorts of ways

out to breakfast [1990s] (orig. US) crazy, eccentric, weird; intoxicated by drink or drugs

Animal Breakfasts

cat's breakfast [1920s+] (Scot./northern) a distasteful mess

cow's breakfast [20C] (Can.) a large straw hat

dingo's breakfast [1960s+] (Aus.) 'a piss and a look around'

donkey's breakfast [late 19C–1910s] 1 a straw hat. 2 (Aus./US) a straw palliasse

have larks for breakfast/supper [1910s] (Ulster) to be especially eloquent

mule breakfast [1920s–40s] (US) a straw hat

rough as a dog's breakfast [20C] (Aus./N.Z.) uncouth, ill-mannered

Fun for Breakfast

breakfast of champions [1990s] 1 the labia. 2 mutual oral-genital stimulation. 3 (US drugs) crack cocaine (pun on the slogan for the US breakfast cereal, Wheaties, long celebrated as 'the breakfast of champions')

Cockney breakfast (UK underworld) gin or brandy and soda water

cockney's luxury [late 19C–1950s] breakfast in bed and using the pot for defecation, rather than leaving the warm house for a trip to the outdoor privy

have a kipper for breakfast [1990s] to have sexual interourse first thing in the morning

jockey's breakfast [1990s] (Irish) sexual intercourse and a slice of bacon

Kentucky breakfast [late 19C+] (US) **1** popularly defined as 'three cocktails and a chew of terbacker'. **2** a bottle of bourbon, a three-pound steak and a setter dog (the dog is there to eat the steak)

Judicial Breakfasts

breakfast uptown [20C] (orig. US Black) a night in jail

have a hearty-choke for breakfast [late 18C–late 19C] to be hanged, also ext. as **have a hearty-choke for breakfast with caper sauce**; thus **artichoke and an oyster**, a pre-hanging breakfast

have claws for breakfast [mid-19C] to be whipped with the *claws* of the cat-o'-nine-tails

take a vegetable breakfast [18C–19C] to be hanged (the punning reference is to a **hearty-choke**)

tip the claws/scroby for breakfast [18C–mid-19C] to be whipped as a judicial punishment (the ety. of *scroby* is uncertain)

No-Breakfast Breakfasts

barber's breakfast [1960s+] (N.Z.) a cough or dry retch, a glass of water and a cigarette (*barber* = shearer)

bushman's breakfast [late 19C+] (Aus.) variously: a look around and a cough/a yawn, a stretch, a piss and a look round/a drink of water and a good look around/a hitch in the belt and a good look around/a shave and a shit and a good look around

---

Awkward Social Situations No. 2

What to Say when One's Companion or Oneself Breaks Wind

a little more choke and ya would've started [20C] (Aus.)

an empty house is better than a bad tenant [1930s+] (N.Z.)

do you spit much with that cough? [1910s–20s] (Can.)

good evening, vicar [20C]

he who smelt it, dealt it [1960s+] used to disclaim all responsibility for having farted

it's the beer/whisky/drink/liquor talking [1920s+] the excuse, usu. in a public house, for breaking wind

who cut the cheese? [1950s+]

drover's breakfast [1940s+] (Aus.) a look around and a
cough

Mexican breakfast [1940s+] (US, Texas) a cigarette and a glass
of water

pommy's breakfast [1990s] (Aus.) a cup of tea and a
cigarette

Spitalfields' breakfast [mid-19C] a tight necktie and a short
pipe (ref. to the impoverished *Spitalfields* area of London's
East End)

BREAKING WIND

blow off [20C]

blow one's horn [20C] (US)

break the sound barrier [1960s+] (Can.)

burn bad powder [1910s–20s]

burst at the broadside [late 17C–mid-19C]

crack a fart [1980s+] (US campus)

cut a finger [late 19C–1900s]

do one's no-manners [1980s]

drop a beast [1970s+] (UK society)

drop a thumper [1960s+]

drop one [1990s] (Aus.)

drop one's guts [1990s]

horse and cart [1970s] (rhy. sl.)

let a badger loose [1990s]

let go a razzo [19C]

let one go (also **let one fly**, **let one off**, **let one rip**) [late 19C]

open one's lunchbox (also **drop one's lunch**) [1990s+]

open one's purse [1990s] (gay)

open the sandwich box [1990s] (Aus.)

shoot bunnies [1990s]

Stepping on a Carpet Frog

Oops

draw mud from the well [1990s] to expel a small amount of faeces when breaking wind

drop a pebble [1990s] as above

float an air biscuit [1990s] to break wind silently, but with a pervasive odour

he thinks his shit don't stink, but his farts give him away [20C] (Aus.)

silent but deadly (also **silent but violent**) [1950s+] a silent, but very smelly, breaking of wind

strike up the colliery band [1990s] to break wind loudly

squeeze the cheese [1990s]

step on a carpet frog [1990s]

strain one's twattling-strings [early 17C–mid-18C]

wind the horn [17C]

C

CARING, NOT *See* **FRANKLY, MY DEAR, I DON'T GIVE A DAMN**

CHILDREN

all white and spiteful [20C] said of a child that, long past its bedtime, has become irritatingly fractious

little rabbits have big ears [20C] said when one is talking indiscreetly in front of children

monkey see, monkey do [1920s+] used to warn someone to stop what they are doing since a bystander, usu. an impressionable child, might be looking and subsequently imitating

Mrs Kelly wouldn't let young Edward play with you [1920s+] (Aus.) addressed to a very dirty or badly behaved child (the *Kellys* in question being the bushranger Ned (1854–80) and his mother)

when you were just a dirty look (also **when you were running up and down your father's backbone, when your mother was cutting bread on you**) [1920s+] (Aus.) i.e. a very long time ago

who slept in the knifebox? [20C] a rhetorical question asked of a child who is making cheeky or impertinent comments

Bastards

To be born an illegitimate child is to …

– **be born on the wrong side of the blanket** [18C]

– **have calluses on one's feet** [20C] (US) describing a child that is born less than nine months after its parents were married; such a child has calluses from making the usual nine-month 'journey' in a somewhat shorter time

be past dying of her first child, [mid–late 17C] of a woman, to have given birth to an illegitimate child

you couldn't throw your hat over the workhouse wall [1900s–30s] used to tease someone who has, or allegedly has, a number of illegitimate children (such children were usually sent to the workhouse)

COITUS INTERRUPTUS

fire one across the bows [1990s]

leave before the gospel [20C] (the image is of leaving before the church service is fully over)

make a coffee house of a woman's cunt [late 18C] i.e. 'to go in and out and spend nothing' (Grose 1796)

Excuse Me, Ma'am, This is My Station

There are a series of expressions for performing coitus interruptus that involve getting off at the railway station before the main one; where this is varies depending on one's geographical location.

Thus, **to get off/out at …**

– **Broadgreen** [20C] (Broadgreen is the station before Edge Hill, which is the station before Liverpool Lime Street)

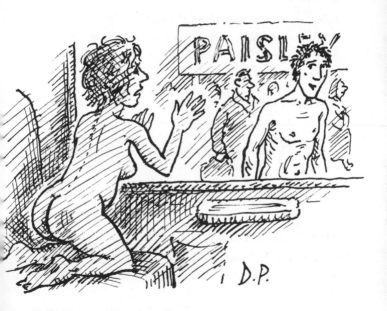

Getting off at Paisley

- **Edge Hill** [20C] (Edge Hill is the station before Liverpool Lime Street)

- **Fratton** [20C] esp. used by sailors based in Bristol (Fratton is the stop immediately before Bristol dockyard)

- **Gateshead** [20C] esp. used by natives of Newcastle-upon-Tyne (Gateshead is the railway station before Newcastle-upon-Tyne)

- **Haymarket** [20C] (Haymarket is the railway station immediately preceding Edinburgh Waverley)

- **Hillgate** [1970s+] (a real or notional bus-stop, immediately before one's actual destination)

- **Paisley** [20C] (used by Glaswegians, where Paisley is the railway station immediately preceding their own)

- **Redfern** [1970s+] (Aus.) (Redfern is the railway station immediately before Sydney Central)

COMPARISONS, MISCELLANEOUS

See also SIMILES, SUNDRY

all behind like a fat woman [20C] tardy, dawdling, slow

all tits and teeth like a third-row chorus-girl [20C] said of a woman who capitalizes on her physical charms

as flat as a shit carter's hat [20C] (Aus.) describing the landscape

as funny as a fart in an elevator/space suit/sleeping bag [20C] (Aus.)

as happy as a penguin in a microwave [1980s+] i.e. unhappy

as many faces as a churchyard clock [20C] used of anyone seen as duplicitous or unreliable

All Tits and Teeth

awkward as a Chow on a bike [1920s+] extremely clumsy

better than a shit in the dark [20C] (Aus.) better than nothing at all

black as a bull's backside [1980s+] (N.Z.) extremely black, usu. of darkness

busy as a body louse [mid-17C–late 19C] very busy

busy as a hen with one chick [17C+] very fussy, extremely punctilious

busy as a one-armed paper-hanger with hives [late 19C+] (orig. Aus./US) exremely busy

camp as a row of (pink chiffon) tents [1950s+] of a male homosexual, ostentatiously effeminate

clumsy as a cub-bear handling his prick [20C] (Can.) very clumsy

cold as a cocksucker's knees [1950s+] (Aus.) of temperature, extremely cold

cold as a mother-in-law's breath [1950s+] (Aus.) of the climate or of a person's emotions, very cold

crooked as a dog's hind leg [late 19C+] very dishonest

cunning as a dead pig [early–mid-18C] very stupid (i.e. not cunning at all)

cunning as a shithouse rat [1960s+] (orig. Aus.) very cunning

demure as a whore at a christening [early 18C+] extremely demure and well-behaved

dry as a dead dingo's donger [1960s+] (Aus.) of weather or one's throat, extremely dry

dry as a Pommie's bath-mat/towel [1980s+] extremely dry (from the belief that English immigrants do not wash)

fine as a cow turd stuck with primroses [late 18C] excellent, first-rate, very fine

fine as a fairy's fart [20C]

fine as wine (US Black) [1970s+] ref. to any particularly attractive male or female

good as a shoulder of mutton for a sick horse [mid-16C–mid-18C] absolutely useless

happy as a boxing kangaroo in fog time [20C] (Aus.) very discontented, very unhappy

happy as a flea at a dog show [1990s+] (N.Z.) very happy

happy as a sick eel on a sandspit [1940s+] (N.Z.) very unhappy

harder than pulling a soldier off your sister [20C] very difficult indeed

have more kid in him than a goat in the family way [1930s+] (Aus.) to be an incurable joker or 'kidder'

his head was so far up his arse if he farted he would whistle [20C] (Aus.)

holding on like death to a dead cat/African/nigger [early 19C–1920s] (US)

holding on like grim death [early 19C+] (orig. US)

hot as a fresh-fucked fox in a forest fire [1950s+] (US) extremely hot, whether as to temperature or sexuality

last as long as a fart in a blizzard [20C] (Aus.)

lower than a snake's belly [1930s+] (Aus.) as low as one can go

mopey as a wet hen [20C] (Aus./N.Z.) miserable, gloomy

quiet as a wasp in one's nose [late 17C] restless, nervy, tense

rough as a badger's arse [late 19C+] bristly, straggly, coarse, also fig. use

rough as a pig's breakfast [20C] (Aus./N.Z.) uncouth

scarce as rocking-horse shit [20C] (Aus.) very rare

silly as a hatful of arseholes [1940s–50s] (Aus.) extremely silly

slick as greased snake shit [20C] (Aus.)

soft as a whore-lady's heart [late 19C–1910s] very hard-hearted

solitary as a bastard on Father's Day [20C] (Aus.) extremely lonely

square as a billiard ball [1940s–50s] (Aus.) anything but honest or 'square', whether morally, sexually or otherwise

thick as fiddlers in hell [20C] (US) very plentiful

thick as glue [19C] very intimate

thick as three in a bed [early 19C] very intimate

thick as two Jews on payday [late 19C] very close (racial stereotyping)

tight as a mouse's earhole [1950s+] of a vagina, very tight

tighter than a witch's/nun's cunt [20C] extremely tight-fitting

COMPLETELY, THOROUGHLY, ENTIRELY, UTTERLY

from arsehole to breakfast table [1940s+] (N.Z.)

from asshole to appetite [late 19C+] (orig. Aus.)

from soup to nuts [late 19C+] (US)

hook, line and sinker [mid-19C+] often ext. to **hook, line, bob and sinker**; sometimes shortened to **hook and line**

Right up to ...

- a fare-thee-well (also **to a fare-you-well, to a fare-ye-well**) [20C] (US)
- **the balls** [1930s+] (US)
- **the ears** [late 19C–1950s] (Aus./US)
- **the handle** [mid-19C] (US)

---

neck and crop [19C] bodily, completely

period, point blank [1930s+] (US)

rump and stump [late 19C–1900s] (Yorks. dial.)

up to one's eyeballs (also **up to one's eyes, up to one's eyebrows, up to the two eyes**) (Aus./US) completely full, as much as is bearable

up to the arse/ass in [mid-19C+] (orig. US) completely overwhelmed by

CONFUSED See DAZED AND CONFUSED

COWARDS AND WEAKLINGS

See also BRAGGADOCIO; BRAVERY

built like a brick shithouse [1920s+] (Aus.) weak (sarcastic usage)

can't beat time on a big drum [1950s] (Aus.)

can't mash ants [1920s–50s] (W.I.)

couldn't …

– **blow the froth off a glass of beer** [1980s] (Aus.)

– **knock/pull a sick moll off a pisspot** [1950s+] (Aus.)

– **knock the dags off a sick canary** [1980s] (Aus.)

– **knock the skin off a rice-pudding** [1980s]

fat around the heart [1930s] (US Black)

n.b.a. [2000s] (US Black) i.e. '*no balls at all*'

no bottle [20C]

nothing to the bear but his curly hair [1930s–40s] (US Black)

valiant as an Essex lion [17C–19C]

you are none of the Hotspurs [early 18C–mid-19C] (*Hotspur* was the nickname of the fiercely brave Harry Percy (1364–1403), son of the Earl of Northumberland, who plays a part in *Henry IV Part One* (1597) by William Shakespeare)

CRIME AND THE UNDERWORLD

See also DRUGS, DOING; HANGED, TO BE; PRISON; VIOLENT AND UNTIMELY END, TO BRING ABOUT A

blood in, blood out [20C] (US underworld) meaning that to join a street or prison gang you must kill, and you may leave it (other than finishing your sentence if in jail) only by being killed yourself

check it in [1990s] (US Black) used by a mugger to his or her victim, when demanding that they hand over money, valuables etc.

come it as strong as a horse [early–mid-19C] (UK underworld) to turn King's/Queen's evidence

An Attempt to Blow the Froth off a Glass of Beer

do you drink? [1960s+] (UK underworld) a coded invitation by a criminal to a police officer whom they are hoping to bribe

draw a thimble [mid-19C] (UK underworld) to steal a pocket watch

fat's a-running [late 19C] (UK underworld) a phr. used to indicate that a loaded van is passing along the street and may be robbed, to the greatest possible extent, by opportunists

flaggin', saggin' and braggin' [1990s+] (US Black gang) used to identify oneself as a member of a gang, esp. in prison

gentleman of three ins [late 18C] 'In debt, in gaol, and in danger of remaining there for life; or, in gaol, indicted and in danger of being hanged in chains' (Grose 1796)

go to/hit the mattress/mattresses [1970s+] (orig. US underworld) to hide, to take refuge, esp. when under siege from another gang (from the practice of sleeping on mattresses in one's hide-out, rather than in one's bed at home. Orig. a US Mafia usage, the phr. was widely popularized by the success of Mario Puzo's book *The Godfather* (1969) and the films that followed)

go out like a sucker [1980s+] (US Black) to die as a result of one's involvement in gangs, drug use and similar activities

half-flash and half-foolish [early 19C] (UK underworld) one who exists on the fringes of the underworld and pretends to a far greater involvement than they actually have

have the game without the name [20C] (US underworld) to have benefits or gains that, while illegally obtained, are seen as worth the poor reputation such actions might engender

if you can't do the time, don't do the crime [20C] (orig. underworld) don't take an action if you cannot deal with the concomitant responsibilities

it looks like rain [20C] (UK/US underworld) an arrest, poss. of the speaker, seems likely

knock the lobb [late 18C] break and enter

knock a peter [1920s+] break into a safe (*peter* = safe, cash-box)

light a candle [late 18C–mid-19C] (UK underworld) leave a public house surreptitiously without paying one's bill

mill a go [late 18C] to succeed in a robbery or theft

Mr Knap is concerned [early 19C] (UK underworld) this is a matter involving theft (from *knap*, to steal)

on a pension [1970s+] (UK underworld) used of a policeman receiving regular bribes

on the plastic [1970s+] (UK underworld) using stolen credit cards for a variety of frauds and swindles

quodding dues are concerned [early 19C] (UK underworld) it is a matter that will involve imprisonment

s.a.n. man [1970s+] (US prison) someone who is dangerous and violent; i.e. 'a *s*top *a*t *n*othing man'

shoe-leather! [mid-19C] (UK underworld) a warning cry uttered by a thief to his confederate on sighting the police

sing like a canary [1950s+] (UK underworld) to make a full confession to the police

standing on the top step [1940s–50s] (UK underworld) used of a man on trial who is facing the likely prospect of a maximum sentence

take tea with someone [late 19C+] (UK underworld) to outsmart a clever person or to defeat someone in authority (from the colonial usage *take tea with*, to associate with, esp. when the relations are mainly hostile)

the music's paid [late 17C–early 19C] (UK underworld) a term used among highwaymen to signify that an individual is a friend and must not be hindered on their journey

trigging the jigger [early 19C] (UK underworld) placing a small piece of paper (the *trig*) in the frontdoor keyhole of a house that is presumed to be uninhabited. If the paper is still there a day later, the robber can presume that the house is empty and can be broken into safely

Police and Underworld Acronyms

a.c.a.b. [1940s+] *a*ll *c*oppers *a*re *b*astards (a popular tattoo in the UK, esp. among Hell's Angels and other 'outlaw' groups)

a.p.b. [20C] (US police) a general alert, a search for a missing person; i.e. *a*ll *p*oints *b*ulletin, a general alert broadcast to all officers and vehicles

b and e [1950s+] *b*reaking and *e*ntering

b.o.s. [1990s] (US, Puerto Rican gangs) a *b*eating *o*n *s*ight

c.c. [20C] (US underworld) the condemned cells; i.e. '*c*ondemned to *c*apital punishment'

c.c.m. [1990s] (US Black) *c*old *c*ash *m*oney

c.c.w. [20C] (US police/underworld) *c*arrying a *c*oncealed *w*eapon

D.O.A. [1970s+] to die before one arrives at a hospital (orig. police jargon, *d*ead *o*n *a*rrival)

K.A.B.G.N.A.L.S. [late 19C] backslang; the word itself is *backslang* spelt backwards and its use – spoken very quickly – is a coded way of asking, 'Do you understand backslang, and shall we use it for this conversation?'

p.i.n.s. [1960s+] (US prison) *p*ersons *i*n *n*eed of *s*upervision

D

DAZED AND CONFUSED

See also MAD; STUPID

all at sea [late 19C+] muddled, confused

all in a twitter [late 18C+] nervous, worried

all of a tiswas [1940s+] (orig. RAF) utterly confused, very excited (? from *tizz*, panic)

all over the place [1920s+] in a great mess, utterly disorganized

all over the placc like a mad woman's shit [1950s+] (Aus.) confused, extremely messy

arse about face [late 19C+] back-to-front

arseholes to breakfast time [late 19C+] (Aus.) totally confused, very chaotic

ass-end-to [20C] in confusion

ass-side-before [20C] head-over-heels

All Over the Place like a Mad Woman's Shit

backbone to breakfast time [1900s] (US) very unsatisfactory, totally confused, chaotic

clear as mud [mid-19C+] completely unclear

devil to pay and no pitch hot [18C+] a mess, a chaotic situation

east and west (also **east, west and crooked**) [20C] (US) disorderly, confused

haul and pull [20C] (W.I.) messy, confused, upset

hell west and crooked/winding (also **high, west and crooked**) [19C+] (orig. US) in a state of disarray, confusion

ho gya/ho-gya/hogya [mid–late 19C] (Anglo-Ind.) in trouble, confused, lost for words, esp. in anglicized phr. **that won't hogya**, that won't do

in a box [mid-19C+] in difficulties, in a confused state of mind, in a quandary

in a Portuguese pignot [1940s] confused, esp. of one who is telling a story but constantly loses their thread

not know if one/someone is Arthur or Martha [20C] **1** used to describe a man who is ambivalent about his sexuality. **2** to be confused as to someone's aims and intentions

off one's base [late 19C+] insane, crazy, confused, muddled, mistaken

off the hinges [17C–18C] physically indisposed, mentally confused

on the hog (train) [late 19C+] out of order, chaotic

out of synch [1970s+] confused, out of touch

thick in the clear [mid-19C] confused

DEATH *See* **DEPARTING THIS LIFE; HANGED, TO BE; VIOLENT AND UNTIMELY END, TO BRING ABOUT A**

DEFECATION

See also DOO-DOO, BEING IN DEEP; EUPHEMISMS; URINATE, TO; VOMIT, TO

Having a Crap

(Popularly from Thomas *Crapper*, 19C manufacturer of water closets, but actually a mixture of Dutch *krappen*, to pluck off, cut off or separate + Old French *crappe*, waste or rejected matter)

back one out [20C] (Aus.)

build a log cabin [1990s] (orig. US campus)

bury a quaker [18C–19C] (a quaker is 'long, thin and wears brown')

choke a darkie (also **strangle a darkie**) [1960s+] (Aus.)

chuck a turd [19C+]

curl one off [1990s+]

despatch one's cargo [1910s–20s]

drop one's bundle [late 19C+]

drop one's load [mid-19C+]

drown the brown turtle [1990s]

give birth to a politician/to your twin [20C] (Aus.)

go and sing 'sweet violets' [20C]

go grunts [1960s]

go to quat [19C] (possibly from *squat*)

have a Brad Pitt [1990s] (rhy. sl.)

have a clear-out [1920s+]

have a dump [1950s–60s]

have an Eartha (Kitt) [1950s+] (rhy. sl.)

have a poo [1950s+]

have a poop [early 18C+]

have a poo-poo [1960s+]

have a shit haemorrhage [1950s] i.e. to be absolutely terrified

heave a Havana [1990s]

kangaroo it [1920s+] (Aus.)

lay a log [1970s+]

open the bomb-bay doors [1990s]

park a darkie [1990s]

park one's fudge [1990s]

pinch a loaf [1990s]

piss backwards [late 19C–1900s]

post a letter [20C]

set a black bass free (also **let go a black bass**) [1990s]

shit bricks [1950s+] i.e. to tremble with fear

A Black Bass Goes Free

– **a job/jobbie** [late 19C+]

– **a job for oneself** [20C]

– **a rear** [20C] (orig. campus)

– **a shit** [mid-19C+]

– **big jobs** [20C] (orig. US juv.)

– **one's business** [late 19C+]

– **one's dirty** [1970s] (US)

– **one's duty** [20C]

squeeze one's head [20C]

take a squat [1930s+]

Alfresco Relief

To do as bears do in the woods is to:

do a rural [20C]

do an agricultural [20C]

go for a walk with a spade [20C]

pick a daisy/the daisies [mid-19C+]

Uncomfortable Excrementitious Circumstances

bake it [late 19C+] to refrain from visiting the lavatory, however desperate the need

dump one's change [1980s+] (US Black/drugs) to excrete
bags of drugs after swallowing them when facing a police
search

shit oneself [1960s+] to defecate in one's underclothes

shit a brick [late 19C+] to defecate after a lengthy period of
constipation

there's a brown dog barking at the back door [20C] (Aus.)
i.e. I need to go soon

Images in Excrement from Oz

**he's that lousy, he'd eat a yard of shit and complain it was an
inch short**

he wouldn't say shit if he had a mouthful i.e. he is the quiet
type

she's had shit thrown at her through a fly-wire door i.e. she
has freckles

**shit stinks, eggs don't bounce and you can't buy generals in a
general store** an answer to the question 'Whaddya know?'

so hungry I'd eat a shit sandwich, only I don't like bread

DEPARTING THIS LIFE

That is ...

when the maggot bites [early 17C–late 19C]

See also HANGED, TO BE; VIOLENT AND UNTIMELY END, TO
BRING ABOUT A

To Pop One's Clogs

answer the last muster/roll-call/round-up [20C]

become a landowner [19C–1900s] (i.e. the owner of a cemetery plot)

bite the big one [1970s+]

bite the dust/chew dust [mid-19C+]

buy it [1920s+]

buy the farm [1950s+] (US) (when pilots of jet fighters crashed on a farm, the government paid enough compensation for the farmer to pay off his mortgage; hence the pilot 'buys the farm' with his death)

call it a day [20C]

call off all bets [1930s–40s] (US Black)

cash in one's checks/chips (also **throw in one's chips, cash one's last check**) [late 19C+] (orig. US)

check in [20C] (US)

check out [1950s+] (orig. US)

chuck a seven [late 19C+] (Aus.) (a throw of *seven* loses one one's stake in the game of craps)

chuck one's hand in [late 19C+]

climb the golden staircase [late 19C] (US)

cock up one's toes [mid-19C]

coil one's ropes [20C] (US)

come down in a pile [20C] (US)

come to a sticky end [1910s+]

cut one's cable [19C]

cut the painter [mid-17C–mid-19C]

Alas, He's Gone ...

– **belly-up** (also **go belly-side up**) [1920s+]

– **conk** [1920s+] (Aus.)

– **the way of all flesh** [late 19C]

– **for his tea** [20C]

– **over the range** [1930s–40s] (Aus.)

– **to grass with his teeth upward** [19C]

– **to shut-eye land** [1940s] (W.I.)

– **to the races** [20C]

– **trumpet-cleaning** [late 19C] (the trumpeter in question being the Archangel Gabriel)

– **up Green River** [mid–late 19C] (US) (from the Green River brand of knife, made in Texas)

– **up Salt River** [1940s] (US Black) to die (? from the salty tears of the mourners and/or the bitterness of death)

– **west** [late 16C+] (from the image of the setting sun, going down in the west + the drive west that took a condemned criminal along Holborn from Newgate prison to the 'triple tree' at Tyburn – today's Marble Arch)

do a oner [1910s+] (Aus.) (death only happens *once*)

do/pull a croak [1900s–20s] (US)

drop off one's/the perch [18C+]

drop off the hook [mid-19C–1920s]

drop off the twig [20C]

feed the fishes [19C+]

finish one's circle [20C] (US) (Western jargon, orig. used of a dead cowman, whose jobs, when alive, included riding the boundaries of the ranch)

finish one's row [20C] (US) (the image is of a ploughman)

fly the coop [mid-19C+] (US)

get one's checks [late 19C] (US)

get the big one [1920s] (US)

get the gun [1900s] (US)

give/make the crow a pudding [late 16C–early 19C] (from *pudding*, entrails, i.e. the crow will eat the entrails of the corpse)

hand in one's dinner pail [1920s+]

hang up one's boots/hat [mid-19C+]

hang up one's fiddle [mid-19C] (US)

have one's number come up [20C]

hit the grit [19C+] (US)

hit/take the deep six [1960s+] (US)

hop the twig [late 18C–early 19C] (UK underworld)

hop the perch [late 19C+]

kick up dust [19C]

kick up one's heels (also **lay up one's heels, topple up one's heels, turn up one's heels**) [late 16C+]

kiss the dust [20C] (orig. US)

lay down one's knife and fork [mid-19C+]

lay up in lavender [late 17C–18C]

leave the minority [late 19C]

lose the number of one's mess [mid-19C]

pass in one's marbles [1900s–50s] (Aus.)

peter out [mid-19C+]

pig out/pork out/pig it [mid-19C]

pip off [1930s] (from the radio 'pips' that signal a time-check)

play the harp [20C] (i.e. in heaven)

poop out [1940s] (US Black)

pop one's clogs/nuts/rocks [1970s+]

punch the clock [1920s+]

Awkward Social Situations No. 3

What to Say to Someone with a Terminal Illness

another clean shirt ought to see you out [1930s+] (N.Z.)

hanging on by your eyelashes, then? [mid-19C+]

on the croak, are we? [late 19C] (US)

Gone for a Burton

[1940s+] (orig. RAF?) dead (the precise ety. remains unknown but there are a number of suggestions: **1** the elision of *burnt 'un*, i.e. a burning aircraft (and its pilot). **2** a euph., going for a glass of *Burton* ale, which ale is heavy, as is a burning aircraft as it crashes to the ground; there was an inter-war advertising campaign for Burton ales, bearing the copy line: 'He's gone for a Burton. **3** *Burton-on-Trent* as rhy. sl. for 'went', as in 'went west'. **4** the tailors Montague Burton: during WW2 the RAF used a number of billiard halls, invariably sited above Burton shops, as medical centres, and those who attended such centres had 'gone for a Burton'. **5** another claim states that Burton's halls were used for morse aptitude tests, not medical check-ups, thus the phr. meant failing such a test. **6** finally seafarers' jargon *burton*, the notoriously unsafe stowing of a barrel athwart rather than fore- and-aft; thus going for a burton meant risking death)

put one's cue in the rack [1980s+]

quit the scene [1950s] (US Black)

shoot one's star [late 19C–1900s]

shuffle off [1920s+] (orig. in *Hamlet* (1602) III.i.67: 'When
    we have shuffel'd off this mortall coile')

snuff it [mid-19C+]

sprout wings [20C] (US)

step off the curb [20C] (US)

stick one's spoon in the wall [19C]

stop ticking [1930s+]

take a dirt nap [1990s] (US Black)

take the big jump [20C] (US)

toss in one's agate [1900s] (Aus.)

turn down one's cup [late 19C] (UK society) (from the old
    habit of turning over one's tea or coffee cup as an indication
    that one no longer wished for it to be filled)

turn one's face to the wall [1940s+]

turn one's toes up/to the daisies [mid-19C+]

In a State of Non-Vitality

burned to the socket [late 17C]

gone for the milk [20C] (Irish)

gone to pot [mid-19C+]

in the grand secret [18C–19C]

on ice [1920s+]

on the blink [late 19C+]

Dead as ...

- **a dodo** [20C]
- **a doornail** [mid-14C–late 16C]
- **a hammer** [19C]
- **a herring** [mid-17C+]
- **a maggot** [1940s+] (Aus.)
- **a tent-peg** [19C–1910s]
- **a wooden Indian** [20C] (US)
- **dogshit** [1980s+]
- **Julius Caesar** [late 19C–1900s]
- **mutton** [late 18C–1910s]
- **small beer** [19C]

on the shelf [19C]
one's race is run [20C]
out of the picture [1940s+]
put to bed with a pickaxe and shovel [19C]
reduced/starved to the last buckle-hole of one's belt [late 19C]
shuffled out of the deck [20C]
tits-up [1960s+] (orig. Can. prison) i.e. laid out on one's back
too full of holes to skin [mid–late 19C] (US) totally riddled
  with bullets
under the daisies [mid-19C+]

under the hatches [late 17C–19C]
under the sod [mid-19C+]
up the spout [early 19C–1920s]
used up [mid-18C–mid-19C]

DEPRESSED

bitched, buggered and bewildered [1930s+]
can't go no further, just like a bear's brother [20C] (US Black)
cheesed off (also **cheesed**) [1940s+]
face as long as a Lurgan spade [late 19C+] (from the Irish
  lorgán spáid, a spade handle) looking miserable
face like a milkman's round [1950s+] as above
face like a yard of pump-water [20C] as above
feeling in low cotton [1940s+] (US)
flat as a tack [1960s+] (Aus.)
fucked up and far from home [1930s+]
in a bad skin [late 18C–1910s]
in bad shape [mid-19C+]
in the cellar [20C]
in the pits [20C]
just like a bear/bear's daughter – ain't got a quarter (also **just
  like the bear's brother, Jim, his pickings are slim**)
  [1920s–40s] (US Black)
look like a wet week [20C] to look utterly wretched
lower than whale shit [20C] (US)

A Shag on a Rock

miserable and lonely as a shag on a rock [1930s+] (Aus.)
miserable as a bandicoot [20C] (Aus.)
not plump currant [late 18C–early 19C]
off one's feed [mid-19C+]
off one's saucer [mid-19C–1900s] (Aus.)
on a downer [1960s+] (orig. US)

on the d.l. [1990s+] (US Black) i.e. '*down low*'

on the downbeat [1940s] (US Black)

on the hog (train) (also **on the pork**) [late 19C+] (US)

out of curl [mid-19C–1910s]

out of one's gears [late 17C–early 18C]

out of one's head [1950s+] (orig. US)

queer/odd as Dick's hatband [18C+]

screwed up [late 19C]

sick as a parrot [1970s+]

under the weather [mid-19C+]

Down ...

– **in one's boots** [20C] (US)

– **in the bushes** [20C] (US)

– **in the cans** [20C] (US)

– **in the chops** [19C]

– **in the gills** [19C]

– **in the dumps** [late 18C+]

– **in the kinks** [20C] (US)

– **in the mouth** (also **down on one's mouth**) [mid-18C+]

– **upon oneself** [early–mid-19C]

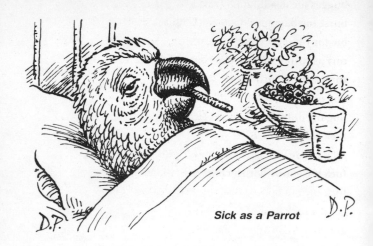

Sick as a Parrot

DISBELIEF, SURPRISE, ANNOYANCE, EXCLAMATIONS THEREOF

See also DISMISSAL AND CONTEMPT; EUPHEMISMS; LEAVE
  ME ALONE; NEGATION, ABSOLUTE; OATHS AND GODLESS
  SWEARING

and did he marry poor blind Nell? [mid-18C–mid-19C]

as if! [1980s+] (Aus./US campus) excl. of disbelief, you must
  be joking

balls, bees and buggery! [late 19C+]

blow me tight! [late 18C–1910s]

boys-a-boys! [20C] (Irish)

bugger me dead! [20C] (Aus.)

burst me bagpipes! [1990s] (US Black teen)

bust my boiler! [20C]

carry me out and bury me decently! [late 18C–mid-20C]

come off the bird-lime! [1910s–20s]

dog my cats! [19C+] (US)

flog my dolphin! [1980s+] (US)

fuck a duck! [1930s+]

fuck me dead/insensible/pink/rigid! [1910s+]

fuck me gently with a chainsaw [1980s+]

fuck my old boots [1940s+]

get the fuck (out of here)! [1950s+]

gracious Miss Agnes! [20C] (US)

great balls of fire! [20C] (orig. US)

great guns and little fishes! [19C+] (US)

hot diggety dog! [1920s+] (US)

I'll eat my hat! [19C+]

I should cocoa! [1930s+] (rhy. sl. *cocoa* = 'say so')

is it buggery! [20C]

I've been to three county fairs and a goat-fucking [1970s+]
(US, mainly South) implying one's astonishment (one has
had many varied experiences, but never one such as this)

'kin'ell! [20C]

kiss me neck! [1950s+] (W.I. Rasta)

knickers to you! [1970s+]

leaping lizards! [1920s–70s] (US)

me elbow! [1910s+] (Irish)

mother of that was a whisker [mid–late 19C] a retort to an utterly implausible story

mule shit! [1920s+] (US)

oingo boingo! [1990s] (S.Afr./US teen)

over the left (shoulder)! [late 17C+]

pickle me bloody agates! (also **pickle me daisy!**, **pickle me tit!**) [1960s+] (N.Z.)

quare man m'da [20C] (Ulster) lit. 'odd man, my father'

says you! [late 17C+]

Well, I'll be ...

- **a (lowdown) son of a bitch!** [20C]
- **a monkey's uncle!** [1920s+]
- **blowed!** [late 19C+]
- **dicked!** [1960s] (US)
- **dipped in shit!** [1960s+] (US)
- **hanged!** [early 18C+]
- **hog-wallered!** [mid-19C+]
- **jiggered!** [mid-19C+]
- **jig-swiggered!** [mid-19C+]
- **jimjammed!** [mid-19C+]
- **switched!** [mid-19C–1940s]
- **torn up for arse-paper!** [1910s+] (N.Z.)

Burst me Bagpipes!

D.P.

shit a brick! [1950s+] (orig. Aus.)

shit the bed! [1990s]

so's your Aunt Tilly/Emma/Fanny [1930s+] (US)

speed the wombats! [1920s+] (Aus.)

stiffen the lizards! [1940s+] (Aus.)

stone me! [1960s+]

strike a light! [1930s+] (orig. Aus.)

strike me perp/perpendicular! [late 19C–1900s]

strip me with the wrought end of a wallaby's dong! [1990s] (Aus.)

stroll on! [1950s+]

tell it to the marines! [early 19C+]

that cock won't fight [19C] used to denigrate the previous statement, 'that won't do', 'you must be joking', 'I'm not having that'

then comes a pig to be killed [late 19C]

thunder and turf! [mid-19C]

what is this, Christmas? [1980s+]

you are Josephus rex [late 18C] you are joking (pun on SE abbr. *jo*, joking + Lat. *rex*, king)

you could have fooled me [1960s+]

you could have knocked me down with a feather [mid-19C+]

your granny! [early 19C+] (US)

your other eye! [20C] (Irish)

What the ...

- **(blue) blazes!** [early 19C+]
- **devil!** [17C+]
- **fuck!** [20C]
- **Hanover!** [1900s–10s]
- **hell!** [early 19C+]
- **Sam Hill!** [early 19C+] (US) (euph. for 'what the hell!')

DISGUSTING

does it smell like cheese to anyone else? [1990s] (US teen) does anyone else think this is totally disgusting, embarrassing, unfashionable etc.?

I have had it up to here [1920s+] I am completely disgusted (with something)

pure nast! [1990s] (US teen) how revolting! (*nast* = nasty)

sick and wrong [1980s+] (US campus) totally disgusting (also used ironically)

state of you! [1980s+] used to express disgust or disbelief at the way somebody is behaving, or at something they said

this gives me the creeps [mid-19C+]

wouldn't it ... [1940s+] (Aus./N.Z.)

– **make you spit chips?**

– **rip yer?**

– rip your ration book?

– rock yer?

– root you?

– rotate you?

– rot yer socks?

DISMISSAL AND CONTEMPT, EXCLAMATIONS THEREOF

See also ABUSE, MISCELLANEOUS; DISBELIEF, SURPRISE, ANNOYANCE; LEAVE ME ALONE

back of my hand (and the sole of my foot) [19C] (Irish/Scot.)

bite my ass! [1950s+] (orig. US)

bite the ice! [1980s] (US teen)

bite your bum! [1950s+] (Aus./N.Z.)

blow it out your ass! [1940s+] (orig. US milit.)

brick wall [1990s] (US teen) i.e. 'I'm ignoring you now'

burrito on your nose! [1990s] (US Black teen) (Mexican-Spanish *burrito*, a tortilla wrapped round a savoury filling, and a US slang term for penis)

d.d.t. [1940s–50s] (US campus) i.e. '*d*rop *d*ead *t*wice'

dieu et mon droit/dright [1910s] a general phr. of self-satisfied dismissal, i.e. don't bother me, I don't care (Fr. *dieu et mon droit*, God and my right, the royal motto of the monarchs of England, adapted as *dieu et mon dright*, rhy. sl. = I'm all right)

dog better than you [20C] (W.I.)

do you see skid marks on my forehead? [1990s] (US campus)
do you think I'm a fool?

eat my lunch! [1990s+]

eat a dick [1990s+] (US Black teen)

eat my shorts [1990s+] (US campus)

five! [1990s] (US teen) the ref. is to the five initial letters of
get out of my face!

fuck that! [20C] often as a comb. e.g., *fuck that for a bowl of
cherries, fuck that for a comic song, fuck that for a top hat*

fuck you, Charley! [19C] often reversed as **Chuck you, Farley!**
(but fooling no-one)

get a life! [1980s+]

Bite Your Bum

Kiss My Tuna

hands off! [mid-16C]

hang it in your ass! [1950s+] (US) often accompanied by a gesture in which the right forefinger is hooked over the left thumb, which in turn makes a circle with the left forefinger

in your dipper! [1920s–30s] (N.Z.)

in your dreams! [1950s+] (orig. US)

in your eye! [late 19C+] (US)

kiss it/me where the sun don't shine! [1940s+]

kiss my arse! [mid-16C+] sometimes ext. as **kiss my ass in Macey's window!** or abbr. to **k.m.a.!**

kiss my parliament! [late 17C]

kiss my tuna! [1980s+] (US teen)

later for that [1940s+] (orig. US Black)

lick my froth! [1980s] (US teen)

lick my love pump! [1980s+] (US campus)

pox take you! [late 16C+]

put/stick it in your ear! [1930s+]

put/stick it where the monkeys shove their nuts [20C] i.e. shove it up your bottom

ram it! (or **ram it up your arsc/ass!**) [1930s⏐] (orig. US)

shove it! [1940s+] (orig. Aus.)

sneck up! [late 16C–early 17C]

suck a fatty! [1990s] (US) i.e. go and suck a *fat* penis

swivel! [1990s] (US teen)

take a run at yourself! [20C] (Aus.)

toast your blooming eyebrows! [late 19C–1910s]

up thine with turpentine! [20C] (US)

up you for the rent! [1930s+] (Aus.)

up your flue! [1970s]

Acronymic Dismissals

f.o. [1940s+] (US) *f*uck *o*ff

f.o.a.d. [1990s+] (US) *f*uck *o*ff *a*nd *d*ie

f.t.w. [1970s+] (US bikers) *f*uck *t*he *w*orld

f.u.b.i.s. [1940s+] *f*uck *y*ou *b*uddy, *I*'m *s*hipping out

g.t.h. [1910s] (US) *g*o *t*o *h*ell

Get ...

- **bent!** [1950s+] (US campus)
- **fucked!** [mid-19C+]
- **lost!** [1940s+]
- **off my case!** [1920s+] (US)
- **out!** [early 18C+]
- **out of here!** [1960s+] (orig. US Black)
- **out of it!** [20C]
- **out of town!** [1980s+] (orig. US Black/campus)
- **ripped!** [1940s+] (Aus.)
- **stuffed!** [1940s+]
- **worked!** [20C] (Aus.)

m.y.o.b. [20C] (US) *m*ind *y*our *o*wn *b*usiness; also extended to **p.m.y.o.b.**, *p*lease...

n.o.y.b. [1910s+] (US) *n*one *o*f *y*our *b*usiness

u.b.d'd! [1910s–20s] *y*ou *b*e *d*amned!

DOO-DOO, TO BE IN DEEP

See also HARM, TROUBLE AND STRIFE

against the collar [mid–late 19C]

all to smash [mid-19C+]

always in trouble like a Drury Lane whore [late 19C+]

balls to the walls [1970s] (US campus) said of a tense or frantic situation that requires the ability to fight back

be in deep doo-doo [1930s+] to be in serious trouble

be in noise [20C] (W.I.)

be had by the short and curlies/shorts/big brown ones/short hair/where the hair is short [1940s+]

come to grief [19C+]

cop a packet [1910s+]

dog dead/dead with you/dead at your door [1940s+] (W.I.)

down on one's luck [mid-19C+]

go up the river [late 19C+]

have one's cock caught in one's zipper [1970s+]

have one's cock on the block [1970s+]

Good Night ...

[late 17C+] used to indicate incipient trouble or one's resignation in the face of a problem or disaster; thus **good night ...**

– **Irene** [1910s+]

– **Joe Doyle** [1930s+] (Irish)

– **McGuinness** [1910s–30s] (N.Z.)

– **nurse** [1910s+]

– **Vienna** [1930s+]

---

have one's tit in a tight crack [1920s+] (Can.)

have one's tit in a wringer [1960s+] (US)

hit the shit [1930s+]

hurtin' for certain [1950s+]

in a pickle/pepper-pot [mid-19C+]

in bad bread/loaf [late 18C]

in for the high jump [1920s+]

in duck's guts [20C] (W.I.)

in guts gully [20C] (W.I.)

in hot ashes [20C]

in huckster's hands [late 18C–19C]

in more shit than a faggot's finger [20C] (Aus.)

in more shit than Ned Kelly [20C] (Aus.) (*Ned Kelly*, 19C Aus. outlaw)

in more trouble than Brown [20C] (W.I.)

Awkward Social Situations No. 4

Things to Say to Someone in Less Happy Circumstances than Yourself

crapaud smoke your pipe [20C] (W.I.)

see you're up arsehole street, mate [1950s+]

your dog's dead [1940s+] (W.I.)

you're toast [1980s+] (US campus)

in shit street [1920s+] (orig. US)

not out of the wood [late 19C+] (orig. US)

on the dink [1900s–10s]

on the mat [late 19C+] (boxing imagery)

on the pot [mid-19C]

on the spot [late 19C]

shit comes in piles [1980s] (US Black) problems always come at the same time rather than one by one

shit out of luck [20C] (US) also abbr. as **s.o.l.**

sur le tapis [mid-19C+] (Fr. 'on the carpet', used in this sense only in English)

under a cloud [early 16C+]

under the cosh/hammer [1950s+]

up a gum-tree (also **up a wattle**) [late 19C+] (orig. Aus.)

up the creek/shit creek (without a paddle) [1930s+]

up the pole [late 19C+]

up to one's ass/ears in alligators/rattlesnakes [1960s+] (US)

In Financial Difficulties

at Staines/the Bush [early 19C] (the *Bush* Inn at *Staines*, once a refuge for debtors)

in Queer Street [early 19C+]

on one's beam-ends [early 19C+] (orig. US)

up King Street [mid-19C–1950s] (Aus.) thus **go up King Street**, to become bankrupt (ref. to *King Street*, Sydney, the site of the Aus. Supreme Court, which hears bankruptcy cases)

In the ...

– **blue** [1920s+]

– **briers** [16C–18C]

– **brook** [late 17C]

– **cactus** [1920s+] (Aus./N.Z.)

– **cart** [late 19C+]

– **cellar** [20C]

– **clart** [1970s] (*clart* = mud)

– **dogfuck** [1970s] (US)

– **doghouse** [1930s+] (orig. US)

– **dwang** [1990s+] (S.Afr.)

– **glue** [1960s+] (US)

– **grease** [1920s–60s] (US)

– **nooer** [1970s] (Aus.)

– **poo** [1960s+] (Aus.)

– **red** [1920s+]

– **shit** (also **in deep shit**) [mid-19C+]

– **soup** [late 19C+] (orig. US)

– **suds** [late 18C–late 19C]

– **tin** [1940s–50s] (Aus.)

– **toot** [1960s+]

DRUGS, DOING

A Variety of Pharmaceutical Phrases

big thing [1970s+] (US) a kilo of cocaine

dead on arrival [1980s+] a brand of heroin

fine stuff [1980s+] marijuana

frisky powder [20C] cocaine

Maui Wowie [1970s+] (US) a potent variety of marijuana, grown in *Maui*, Hawaii

midnight oil [1940–50s] opium

monkey bait [1950s+] free samples of addictive drugs

tumblings and blankct [1920s–40s] tobacco and papers

In the Cactus

Supply and Demand

all right? [20C] a coded query: do you need any drugs?

beam me up, Scotty! [1970s] give me some drugs! (usu. crack cocaine)

do you need a boy? [1960s+] a surreptitious request for heroin

following that cloud [1980s+] (drugs) searching for drugs

good go [20C] the proper amount of drugs for the money paid

hangin', bangin' and slangin' [1990s] (US Black gang) a phr. used to describe the 'gangsta' lifestyle: associating with one's friends and fellow gangsters, fighting with other gangs and selling drugs

hold the bag [mid-18C+] to be in possession of a quantity of drugs, to deal drugs

hurtin' for certain [1950s+] (US Black) in great need, esp. of drugs or sex

on a mission [1990s+] looking for and/or bingeing on drugs

on the bricks/pavement/sidewalk [1930s+] (US) walking the streets searching for drugs

six-up! [1980s+] a warning shout to alert drug-users or illicit street vendors to the presence of the police or security guards; the drugs or merchandise should be hidden or even thrown away to prevent problems in a search

you all set? [1980s+] (US drugs) do you need to buy any drugs?; the response, if one requires nothing, is 'I'm set (for now)'

In or Entering Altered States of Consciousness

all lit up [1960s+] under the influence of drugs (previously meaning under the influence of alcohol)

atop Mt Shasta [20C] (US) addicted to narcotics

bake sale [1980s+] (US) a session of smoking crack cocaine

bending and bowing [20C] (US) experiencing the effects of a drug, esp. heroin

bent out of shape [1960s+] intoxicated by drugs

boot the gong [1950s+] to smoke marijuana

chalked up [1950s+] under the influence of cocaine

Loaded

[late 19C+] synonyms for intoxication by a drug, incl. **loaded to the ...**

– **barrel**
– **earlobes**
– **gills**
– **guards**
– **gunnels**
– **hat**
– **muzzle**
– **plimsoll mark**
– **tailgate**

---

feeling no pain [1920s+] unconcerned, casual; a state achieved with or without drugs

fly Mexican airlines [1960s+] to smoke marijuana

geed-up (also **g'd up**) [1920s–70s] (US) intoxicated by drugs

hit the ceiling [1910s+] (orig. US) to smoke opium

hold one's high (US Black/drugs) to maintain control while intoxicated by alcohol or a drug

hop (someone) up (US) to give an injection (of legal or illegal drugs)

in orbit (also **into orbit**) (orig. US) [1970s+] a state of intoxication from drugs or alcohol

in the ozone [1970s+] (US) intoxicated by drugs or drink

in the spoon [20C] using drugs

night on the rainbow [1940s] a night spent under the influence of drugs

off one's head/bonce/onion/thatch [20C] intoxicated by a drug

on a bender (also **on a bend**) [1970s+] bingeing on drugs

on a high [1940s+] the euphoric, pleasurable state induced by taking drugs

on a jag [late 17C+] out on a spree, orig. used of drinking and later ext. to drugs

on a trip [1960s+] under the influence of drugs

on the hip (also **take it on the hip**) [1920s+] using narcotics, whether opium, heroin or, latterly, crack cocaine

on the hop [1950s] (US) using narcotics

on the needle [1940s+] using narcotic drugs

on the stuff [1920s+] using a narcotic drug, esp. heroin

out of it [1960s+] (orig. US) unable to function adequately because of one's intoxication by drugs or alcohol

out to breakfast [1990s] (orig. US) intoxicated by drink or drugs

out to lunch [1950s+] (orig. US campus) as above

over the hump [1910s+] (US) enjoying the peak of a drug experience

ping-in-wing [1940s–50s] (also **ping-in-the-wing**, **ping-wing**) an injection of a narcotic

psychedelic to the bone [1970s+] (US Black) extremely intoxicated by a drug, but not necessarily an hallucinogen

Out of One's ...

- **box** (also **off one's box**, **off one's pot**) [1960s+]
- **brain** (also **off one's brain**) [1960s+]
- **cranium** [1960s+]
- **face** [1970s+]
- **mind** [1960s+]
- **nut** [late 19C+]
- **skull** [1960s+]
- **tits** (also **off one's tits**) [1970s+]
- **tree** (also **off one's tree**) [1960s+]

ride the white horse (US Black) to be intoxicated with drugs

riding a thorn [1950s] injecting narcotics

riding a/the wave [1920s–40s] under the influence of drugs

riding the witch's broom [1950s] using heroin

ripped to the tits/gills [1970s+] (orig. US) very intoxicated by
   drink or drugs

shoot up [1920s+] to take narcotic drugs by injection

someone blew out his/her pilot light [1970s+] (US campus)
   ref. to anyone considered odd, intoxicated, on drugs etc.

Out of One's Tree

stoned to the eyes/eyeballs [1950s+] (orig. US) very intoxicated from drugs or alcohol

torch up [1960s+] to smoke marijuana.

turn on [1950s+] to take drugs, esp. heroin, morphine or cannabis

wired for sound [1960s+] (drugs) experiencing the most extreme effects of cocaine or amphetamines

---

The Secret Language of Drugs

a.i.p. [1980s+] heroin from *A*fghanistan, *I*ran and *P*akistan.

D.F.F.L. [1950s+] *D*ope *F*orever, *F*orever *L*oaded, a popular patch worn by Hells Angels, hippies, and others

m.m.s [1970s] the hunger that follows smoking marijuana; i.e. '*m*arijuana *m*unchies'

n.h.b [1980s+] the butt end of a cannabis cigarette; *n*asty *h*ot *b*it

o.o.c. [1980s+] (US campus) drunk, high on drugs; i.e. '*o*ut *o*f *c*ontrol'

p.a.b.a.c.a.b. [1980s+] (US) an exhortation to smoke cannabis; *p*ack *a* *b*owl *a*nd *c*atch *a* *b*uzz

q.p. [1980s+] (US) a *q*uarter *p*ound (of cannabis)

s.s. [1930s] a *s*kin *s*hot; i.e. an injection of drugs that does not hit a vein

---

DRUNK, GETTING AND BEING

See also DRUGS, DOING; URINATE, TO; VOMIT, TO

To be Pleasantly Tipsy

be quite the gay drunkard [late 19C]
bright in the eye [late 19C–1920s]
feel good [late 19C+]
fly rather high [mid–late 19C]
have a buzz on [mid-19C+] (orig. US)
have a swelled/swollen head [late 19C+]
have an edge on [late 19C–1960s]
how-come-ye-so [18C]
in a merry pin [late 18C–early 19C]
listing to starboard [19C+]
moist round the edges [1900s–20s]
off nicely [19C]
off the nail [early 19C]
on the tiddley [mid-19C+]
shake a cloth in the wind [late 18C–mid-19C]
slightly tightly [late 19C]
taking it easy [19C]

To Be or Get Quite Merry

about right [19C+]
all at sea [late 19C+]
all mops and brooms [19C+]

Appleton talking (also **Fernandez talking**) [20C] (W.I.) (the brand names of popular rums)

ass on backwards [20C]

away with the band [20C] (Ulster)

be a passenger on the Cape Ann stage [mid-19C] (US campus)

been in the sun [late 18C–late 19C]

below the mahogany [20C]

M'Lud, I was Only Half ...

- **canned** [1920s+]
- **cocked** [20C]
- **fonged** [1940s+] (N.Z.)
- **gassed** [1910s+]
- **high** [20C] (US)
- **in the bag** [1940s+] (orig. US)
- **nelson** [1920s]
- **pissed** [20C]
- **rats** [late 19C]
- **rinsed** [1910s+] (Aus./N.Z.)
- **screwed** [mid-19C+]
- **shot** [mid-19C+] (orig. US)
- **slewed** [early 19C+]
- **tore** [20C] (Ulster)

bet one's kettle [20C]

booed and hissed [1980s] (rhy. sl. 'pissed')

Brahms and Liszt (also **Mozart and Liszt**) [1920s+] (as above)

break one's leg [mid-19C]

burn one's shoulder [20C]

carry a turkey on one's back [19C]

carrying a load [20C]

catch/get the flavour [19C]

come from Liquorpond Street [early 19C–1900s]

cop the brewery [mid-19C–1900s]

dead to the (wide) world (also **out to the wide**) [late 19C+]

down by the head [19C]

drive the brewer's horse [19C]

fallen off the wagon [20C]

feeling right royal [late 19C+]

flying blind/ high [20C]

get/have a skinful [late 18C+]

get a snootful [1910s+]

go Borneo [1970s+] (US campus)

go for veg [1970s] (US campus) (i.e. one becomes a *veg*etable)

go to Mexico [1950s+] (US)

go to Putney (on a pig) [mid-19C]

half seas over [late 17C+]

half the bay over [late 19C]

half-half-and-half [late 19C]

half-shaved [early–mid-19C] (US)

On ...

- **a bat** [mid-19C+] (orig. US)
- **sentry** [late 19C–1910s]
- **the floor** [20C]
- **the fritz** [20C]
- **the grog** [1950s+]
- **the juice** [1950s+]
- **the mop** [19C+]
- **the ooze** [1920s+]
- **the ran-tan** [early 18C–mid-19C]
- **the scoop/scoot** [1900s–10s] (Aus.)

hand and fist [20C] (rhy. sl. 'pissed')
have a hummer going [1960s+] (US)
have a smell/sniff of the barman's/barmaid's apron [1920s+]
have ballast on board [late 19C+]
have malt above the water [19C]
have one's eyes opened [20C]
have one's little hat on [18C]
have one's pots on [19C]
have one's sails high [1940s–50s] (US Black)
have the sun in one's eyes [mid-19C]
high as a cat's back [mid-19C+] (US)

high as a fiddler's fist [1950s–60s] (US)

high as Lindbergh [1930s–40s] (US) (Charles *Lindbergh*, the aviator who was the first to fly the Atlantic solo)

hit and missed [1960s+] (rhy. sl. 'pissed')

in good/proper fettle [late 19C–1910s]

in la-la land [1980s+] (US)

in one's cups [early 18C+]

in the bag/wrapper [1940s] (orig. US) thus **half in the bag**, beginning to become drunk

---

Comparatively Cut: Drunk as ...

- **a (fresh-)boiled owl** [late 19C+] (orig. US)
- **a duck (and don't give a fuck/quack)** [1910s+]
- **a pissant** [1930s+] (Aus.)
- **a polony** [late 19C]
- **a rat** [19C+]
- **an emperor** [late 18C]
- **Chloe** [early 19C+]
- **cooter brown** [1900s–40s] (orig. US Black)
- **David's sow** [late 17C+]
- **dogshit** [1980s+]
- **floey** [late 19C–1900s]

---

laid to the bone [1960s–70s] (US Black)

lit to the gills [20C]

look through a glass [19C]

looking lively [mid-19C+]

lord and mastered [20C] (rhy. sl. 'plastered')

lose one's rudder [20C]

low in the saddle [20C] (orig. US)

lush it around/up [1950s+] (US)

nicely, thank you [1920s–50s]

off one's bean [20C]

off one's nut [mid-19C+]

one over the eight/nine [1920s+] (orig. UK milit.) (the numbers refer to the supposedly 'safe' quantity of pints of beer)

open a keg of nails [1930s] (US)

out of one's head [1950s+] (orig. US)

over the bay [late 18C–late 19C] (US)

over the line [1920s]

over the plimsoll [1920s+] (N.Z.)

overheat one's flues [late 19C]

peek through one's liquor [1930s–40s] (US Black) to pose as sober when one is in fact drunk

row up Salt River [early 19C–1940s] (US)

see Indians [19C] (US)

see the lions [mid-19C+]

shot full of holes [1910s+] (Aus./N.Z.)

shot in the neck [early–mid-19C] (US)

A Fresh-Boiled Owl

shout oneself hoarse [late 19C–1900s]

take in a cargo [early 19C]

three sheets in the wind (also **three sheets to the wind, three sheets over, one/two/four/six sheets to the wind**) [mid-19C+] (nautical imagery: a sailing ship carrying 'three sheets [sails] to the wind' is top-heavy)

too many cloths in the wind [late 19C]
tore out of the frame [1970s] (US campus)
under the weather [mid-19C+]
wave a flag of defiance [late 19C–1910s]
worse for wear [20C]
wrong all round the corner [late 19C–1920s]

To be Unforgivably Guttered

banged up to the eyes [mid-19C–1920s]
be in on one's fourth [late 19C–1900s]
bent out of shape [1960s+]
blue-blind paralytic [1910s] (Aus.)
burn with a low blue flame [1960s+]
can't say 'British constitution' [late 19C]
can't say 'naval intelligencer' [20C]
can't see a hole in a forty-foot ladder [late 19C+]
come home by rail [1930s+] (Aus.) to be so drunk that one
   can only proceed by hanging onto things
commode-hugging drunk [1970s+] (US campus)
down among the dead men [mid-19C]
drown the shamrock [20C] (Irish) to get very drunk on
   St Patrick's day
drunk to the pulp [1970s] (US Black)
fried to the gills/tonsils [1920s+]
full to the bow-tie [1950s]
full to the bung [mid–late 19C]

full to the gills [1910s+] (orig. US)

get one's nose painted [20C]

get one's shoes full [20C]

get one's soul in soak [19C]

go to bed in one's boots [late 19C–1900s]

have a beer in [1900s] (N.Z.)

have a brick in one's hat [mid–late 19C] (orig. US)

have a load on [late 19C+]

have all that/more than one can carry [mid-18C+]

have breath strong enough to carry coal [late 19C] (orig. US)

have one's back teeth afloat/have one's teeth swimming [late 19C+]

have one's kidneys afloat [late 19C+]

higher than a Georgia pine [1930s–40s] (US Black)

hog-whimpering (drunk) [20C] (US)

iced to the eyebrows [20C]

in a terrible state of chassis [1920s+] (Irish)

in one's royal [20C] (W.I.)

in the ditch [1980s+] (US)

knee-walking drunk [1970s+] (US)

lit up like Broadway/Main Street/Times Square [20C]

maxed out [1970s+]

not able to hit the ground with his hat [20C] (US)

out of one's kug [1960s] (US)

pissy-arsed [20C]

pissy-drunk [20C] (US)

play camels [late 19C] (Anglo-Ind.) (from the *camel's* ability to hold liquids)

ripped out of one's gourd [1980s+] (US campus)

smash hell through a gridiron [late 19C] (US)

so drunk that he opened his shirt collar to piss [19C]

stewed as a prune [1920s+]

stewed to the gills/ears/eyeballs/eyebrows [1920s+]

swallow a hare [late 17C–early 19C]

tanked to the wide [late 19C+]

tight as an owl [late 19C+] (US)

tight as a drum/fart [20C]

tired and emotional [1960s+]

torn out of the frame [1970s] (US campus)

Pissed as ...

– **a chook** [1960s+] (N.Z.)

– **a fart** [20C]

– **a newt** [20C]

– **a parrot** [1990s] (Aus.)

– **a rat** [20C]

– **arseholes** [1960s+]

---

under the table [mid-19C+]

walk on one's cap-badge [1910s+] (orig. milit.)

watch the ant races [1970s+]

whittled as a penguin [1960s] (Aus.)

On Ye Olde Pisse

be among the philistines [late 17C–19C]

bite one's grannam [17C] (from *grannam*, corn, the basic ingredient of some spirits)

bitten by a barn-mouse [late 18C–early 19C]

bitten by the tavern bitch [17C–18C]

bloody flag is out (also **hang out the bloody flag**) [late 17C–early 19C]

bung one's eye [late 18C–19C]

buy the sack [early 18C–early 19C]

chirping merry [late 17C–early 19C]

clip the King's English [late 17C–late 18C] (i.e. one slurs one's words)

crash a bottle [16C]

cut over the head [18C]

drunk with a continuando [late 17C–early 18C] (i.e. for a long time)

eat hull-cheese [17C] (i.e. 'eat' malt liquor and water)

eyes set at eight in the morning [early 17C]

eyes set in one's head [early 17C]

flag of defiance is out [late 17C–early 19C]

go down with barrel fever [18C+]

go to Jericho [late 18C–early 19C]

go to Jerusalem [mid-18C–early 19C]

grectin' fou [17C+] (lit. 'crying drunk')

have a pot in the pate [mid-17C–mid-18C]

have been in the sun [mid-18C]

have bread and cheese in one's head [mid-17C–mid-18C]

have corns in the head [mid-18C–mid-19C]

have malt above the wheat [mid-16C]

have seen the French king [17C]

hit on the head by the tavern bitch [17C–18C]

Hungover

feeling like a stewed monkey [19C] (US)

feeling like a warmed-up corpse [1920s]

with a head like a drover's dog [1940s+] (Aus.)

have a mouth like …

… a lorry driver's crotch [1960s+]

… a nun's minge [1960s+]

… the bottom of a cocky's cage [1960s+] (Aus.)

… the bottom of a parrot's cage [1940s+]

… the inside of an Arab's armpit [1940s+]

… the inside of an Arab's underpants [1940s+]

---

hit under the wing [mid-19C]

hunt a tavern fox [mid–late 17C]

in one's ale/ales [late 16C–early 17C]

in one's altitudes [17C–late 18C]

in one's armour [17C–early 19C]

in one's pots [early 17C]

kill one's dog [mid-18C]

letting the finger ride the thumb [18C]

lose one's legs [mid–late 18C]

making Ms and Ts [late 18C–mid-19C] (punning on 'empty')

needing a reef taken in [19C] (orig. naut.)

powder one's hair [18C]

put another nail in one's coffin [19C]

queer in the attic [19C]

shoe the goose [early 17C]

swallow a tavern token [late 17C–18C]

thumped over the head with Samson's jawbone [19C]

wash one's face in an ale clout [16C–17C]

wear the barley cap [late 16C–late 17C]

wet one's neck [early 19C]

whip the cat [17C]

wrapt up in warm flannel [late 18C–early 19C]

The Secret Language of Drinking

a.b.f. [1910s+] the last drink of a session; i.e. '*a b*loody *f*inal drink'

b and s [mid-19C+] *b*randy and *s*oda; sometimes reversed to **s and b**

B.Y.O. [1960s+] (US/Aus.) *B*ring *Y*our *O*wn; referring to bringing drinks to a party or an unlicensed restaurant

B.Y.O.L. [1920s+] *B*ring *Y*our *O*wn *L*iquor; also (Aus.) **B.Y.O.G.** *B*ring *Y*our *O*wn *G*rog

g and t [20C] *g*in *and t*onic

o.d.v. [mid-19C–1920s] brandy; punning on Fr. *eau de vie*

u.d.i. [1990s] *u*nidentified *d*rinking *i*njury

v.a.t. [1980s+] *v*odka *and t*onic; coined for the TV series *Minder* (1979–81)

EMBARRASSING

See also NERVOUS, ANXIOUS, AGITATED

cringe, cringe, grovel, grovel [1950s+] a phr. used after one has committed some form of embarrassing solecism and wishes to leaven the error with humour

crowd the mourners [mid-19C–1920s] to intensify someone's embarrassment

cut a gut [1920s+] (US) to make an embarrassing mistake

have a crow to pick [16C–18C] to have an embarrassing or contentious subject to discuss

hopping around like a gin at a christening [1960s+] (Aus.) on one's best behaviour, esp. when slightly nervous, socially uncomfortable (*gin* = woman)

make a holy show/spectacle of oneself [late 19C+] (Aus./Irish) to make oneself the cause of a scandal or embarrassment

Awkward Social Situations No. 5

Being Caught ...

– **holding one's dick** [20C] (US)

– **with one's trousers down** [1960s+]

And thus finding oneself ...

in more strife than a pork chop at a synagogue [1950s+] (Aus.)

party foul! [1980s+] (US campus) that was a blunder! how embarrassing! excl. uttered when someone has behaved in a socially unacceptable manner at a party, esp. by vomiting or spilling alcohol

pull down the blind! [late 19C] used to an amorous couple whose activities are embarrassing those around them

pull down your basque! [late 19C] said to a young woman seen as acting with a lack of decorum

q.p. [1990s] (US teen) (Sp. *que pena*, 'how embarrassing')

red/pink in the gills [late 18C+] to be embarrassed

ETIQUETTE

See also AVE ATQUE VALE

mercy buttercups [1980s+] (US campus) thank you (from Fr. *merci beaucoup* 'thank you very much')

screws me [1970s] (US campus) excuse me

seafood plate [1980s] (US campus) please (Fr. *s'il vous plait* 'please')

sieg heil [1970s] (US campus) affirmative response to 'How are you?' (from the Nazi salute)

squeeze me [1990s] (US campus) excuse me

EUPHEMISMS

See also LEAVE ME ALONE; OATHS AND GODLESS SWEARING

abaft the wheel-house [late 19C] (US) just below the small of the back; thus euph. for the buttocks

arrive at the end of the sentimental journey [late 19C–1910s] of a man, to have sexual intercourse (literary euph.; the conclusion of Laurence Sterne's *Sentimental Journey* (1768), in which the narrator obviously retires to bed with a chambermaid)

be at the races [20C] to work as a street-walker (the prostitute's euph. to prying acquaintances)

beautiful pair of brown eyes [1940s–60s] attractive female breasts

bit of how's yer father [1940s+] sexual intercourse (from orig. music-hall use as a 'nudging' euph.)

catch a horse [20C] (Aus.) to urinate

chase a rabbit [20C] (US) as above

cheese and crackers! *excl.* [20C] (US) euph. for *Jesus Christ!*

down there [20C] a coy reference to the vagina

Ethiopian in the fuel supply [20C] a self-consciously

contrived euph. for *nigger in the woodpile* (18C *Ethiopian*, a Black person)

extract the urine [1930s+] (orig. milit.) euph. for *take the piss*

fie for shame [19C] the vagina; from the image of the vagina as something shameful; cf the euph. Lat. *pudendum* (lit. 'that of which one ought to be ashamed')

fond of her mother [1980s+] (gay) homosexual (a 'nudging' euph., emphasising the supposed 'creation' of gay men by their suffocating mothers)

for crying in a cemetery/for crying in the beer [20C] (US) euph. for *for Christ's sake*

four-legged frolic [mid-19C] sexual intercourse

friend of Dorothy [1950s] a homosexual; from the character played by Judy Garland in the 1939 film *The Wizard of Oz* (Garland remains a deity to large parts of the gay world)

gentleman of the back door [18C] a homosexual

get one's hair cut [20C] to visit a woman for sex

gone to visit his uncle [late 18C–19C] of a man who has deserted his wife soon after the marriage (ironic)

go see a man [19C] to take a drink

have an appointment [20C] (US campus) to go out drinking (the euph. excuse offered, usu. to one's wife)

have been after the girls [mid-late 19C] to have contracted a venereal disease

hundred-and-seventy-fiver [1990s] (gay) a homosexual (para. 175 of the German penal code of 1871 outlawed homosexuality)

it's a term of endearment among sailors [20C] euph. for the excl. *bugger!*

When the Shit Hits the Fan ...

when the ca-ca hits the fan [1940s+]

when the doo-doo hits the fan [1940s+]

when the excrement hits the air conditioning [1940s+]

when the omelette hits the fan [1940s+]

when the solids hit the air conditioning [1940s+]

Judas Priest! [1910s+] (orig. US) euph. for *Jesus Christ!*

seduce my ancient footwear [1940s+] euph. version of *fuck my old boots!*

short reply in the plural [20C] euph. for *balls!*

take the kids to the pool [1990s] to defecate

testicles to you! [20C] a ponderous euph. for the coarser *balls to you!*

testicular elevation [20C] a ponderous euph. for the coarser *balls-up*

two ends and the middle of a bad lot *n.* [late 19C] (middle class) a euph. phrase that describes a wholly 'bad lot'

use the windward passage [late 18C–early 19C] to have anal sex

usher of the back door [late 18C–early 19C] a homosexual

visit the bank/take a trip to the bank [20C] to go the lavatory

whole famn damily [20C] whole damn family

EXCELLENT *See* S'WONDERFUL, S'MARVELLOUS

EXHAUSTED

all in but one's shoestrings/bootstraps/shoelaces [20C] (US)

dead on one's feet [late 19C+]

dead on the vine [20C] (orig. US Black)

dead to the curb [1950s] (US Black)

dead to the (wide) world (also **blind to the wide, out to the wide**) [late 19C+] (orig. US)

feel like a ball/bag of string [1950s] (Aus.)

Too Tired to Pull a Greased Stick out of a Dog's Arse

feel like a stewed witch [19C] (US)

Harry flakers [1940s+]

my arse is dragging [1910s+] (orig. US)

on one's knees [1920s+]

on the nod [1930s+]

out for the count [late 19C+]

out of commission [late 19C+]

out of it [20C] (orig. US)

tapped out [1950s+] (US)

too tired to pull a greased stick out of a dog's arse [1980s+]
  (Aus.)

tuckered out [mid-19C+] (Aus./US)

used up [mid-19C+]

FAILURE'S NO SUCCESS AT ALL

bat zero [1920s–50s] (US) to fail completely

born under a threepenny halfpenny planet [17C–19C] a complete failure

come to grief [19C+] to fall into difficulties, to fail (orig. a sporting phr. meaning to fall from one's horse)

down the banks [late 19C] a state of failure

fluff in the pan [mid–late 19C] a failure

give it back to the Indians [20C] (US) used when anything fails or breaks

his name is Dennis [19C+] (US) indicating failure

stinks like hogan's goat [20C] (US) bad, objectionable, a failure etc.

little end of the horn [19C+] (US) failure; usu. in the phr. **come out of the little end of the horn**

not on the same bus [1990s+] (US teen) used of the one person in a group who fails properly to fit in

on a bust [20C] failing, doing badly

someone's name is mud [19C+] implying failure or disgrace following some objectionable or foolish act

so very human [late 19C] (UK society) a generalized (and ironic) excuse for a variety of failings

Wall Street didn't jump [1970s+] (US teen) anything that fails to produce the anticipated and desired excitement from bystanders, let alone produce an effect on the US economy

FARTING *See* **BREAKING WIND**

FASHION *See* **SARTORIAL MATTERS**

FAT AND THIN

Fat as a Boarding-House Pudding

Some colourful expressions from Oz:

an arse like two pigs fighting in a sugar bag

full as a fat lady's knickers/socks

full as a fat man's undies

I've seen better legs on a table

like two bulldogs fighting under a saddle blanket = what a fat woman's behind looks like when she walks in trousers

she's so fat, you'd have to roll her in flour to find the wet spot
(in relation to attempting sexual congress with an obese
woman)
she's so fat, you'd have to slap her in the guts and ride the
waves in
she's two pick handles wide

Skinny: All Cock and Ribs

all cock and ribs like a musterer's dog [1970s+] (Aus./N.Z.)
all prick and ribs like a drover's dog [1960s+] (Aus.)
all ribs and dick like a robber's dog [1990s] (Aus.)
looking like a tooth-drawer [17C]
one of Pharaoh's lean kine [late 16C] (*kine* = cattle)
so thin you can smell shit through him [late 19C]

FLIES *See also* **SLIPS**

Awkward Social Situations No. 7

What to Say to Someone Whose Fly is Open

cheese on your chin [2000s] (Irish)

do you feel a draught/breeze? [20C]

flying low [1990s+] (Irish)

it's one o'clock (at the button factory/waterworks) (also **it's two o'clock, it's three o'clock**) [20C]

showing next week's washing [20C]

the cow barn is open [1960s+]

the garage door is open [1960s–70s] (US)

the hot dog stand is open [20C] (US)

your barn door/gate is open [20C] (orig. US)

your business is open [20C] (US) a statement which elicits the reply, 'Is my salesman in or out?'

your horse is going to get out [20C] (US)

your lunch bucket is open [1970s+] (US)

your nose is bleeding [late 19C+]

FRANKLY, MY DEAR, I DON'T GIVE A DAMN

be like that (see if I care) [1960s+] a dismissive, if petulant (and not wholly sincere) phr. denoting one's refusal to care about another's (injurious) actions

b.f.d. [1970s+] (US) i.e. '*b*ig *f*ucking *d*eal'

care factor zero [1990s] (US teen)

The Horse is Out

fuck you Jack, I'm all right! [late 19C+]

I couldn't give a shit [1970s+]

I should worry [20C]

my troubles! [late 19C+] (Aus.)

my worries! [1950s+] (Aus.)

no hide off my back [1920s+]

not take a blind bit of notice [20C] to have no interest whatsoever, not to care at all

san fairy ann! [1910s+] (orig. milit.) a general excl. of negation, e.g. I don't care! the hell with you! (Fr. *ça ne fait rien*, that's nothing)

stay and be hanged! [late 19C] a general excl. of resigned exasperation, oh all right! see if I care! do what you want!

that's your problem [1960s+] (orig. US)

tough beans! [1960s+] (US) bad luck (not that I care)

tough shit! [1950s+] so what! see if I care! a response indicating little or no sympathy with the first speaker

I Don't Give ...

– **a bugger** [1930s+]

– **a cat's ass** [1990s+] (US)

– **a damn** [18C+]

– **a fiddler's fuck** [1930s+] (orig. US)

– **a hoot** [mid-19C+]

– **a monkey's** [1960s+]

– **a rap (for)** [mid-19C+]

– **a sod** [1960s+]

– **a stuff** [1970s+] (orig. Aus./N.Z.)

– **a toss** [late 19C+]

– **a tuppenny damn/dump/fuck** [late 19C+]

– **rotten apples** [1950s] (US)

– **the sweat off my balls** [1930s+] (orig. US)

I Couldn't Care ...

– **a brass button** [20C]

– **a dead Chinky/two dead Chinkies** [20C] (Aus.)

– **a fiddlestick** [early 19C+]

– **a fig** [mid-17C+]

– **a fouter/footer** [early 17C–late 19C] (Fr. sl. *foutre*, to fuck)

– **a fuck** [1910s+]

– **a hang** [late 19C+]

– **a Pall Mall** [late 19C] (rhy. sl. *Pall Mall* = gal = girl = prostitute)

– **a raas/rass** [20C] (W.I.) (taboo W.I. slang *raas*,? from phr. *your arse* or Du. *raas*, to rage, to rave)

– **a sheep's trotter** [20C] (Aus.)

– **a whoop** [20C] (US)

– **beans** [mid-19C+] (US)

– **less** [1940s+] (UK/US)

– **whether school keeps or not** [mid-19C+] (US)

One may also not care ...

– **a bean/a row of beans**

– **a blast**

– **a blow**

- a bluebag
- a brass farthing
- a bugger/two buggers
- a button/row of buttons
- a cabbage-leaf
- a cent/two cents/a ten cent piece
- a chip
- a condash
- a continental
- a copper
- a cow (as euph. for *fuck*)
- a crap
- a cuss/a curse/a tuppenny cuss/a God's curse
- a damn/a twopenny damn/a D
- a darn/durn
- a dash
- a dime
- a doodle
- a dump
- a fart/a fartful/a tuppenny fart
- a farthing
- a farthing dip/a twopenny dip
- a figleaf
- a fish's tit
- a flash (in hell)
- a groat

- a hair
- a hoot/two hoots
- a jack-rat
- a jot
- a kitty
- a louse
- a mackerel's fur
- a monkey's/two monkeys/a monkey's hang/a monkey's fart
- a motherfuck
- a pin/a pin's head/a row of brass pins
- a point
- a priest's dick
- a rap
- a rat's arse/ass
- a rip
- a rush
- a snap/a snap of the fingers
- a snuff
- a sod
- a sou(s)
- a straw/two straws/three straws
- a stuff
- a sugar
- a thank'ee
- a tinker's curse/cuss/darn/damn
- a tootle

– a toss
– a traneen/thraneen
– a turd
– a twist of a fiddler's elbow
– a twopenny worth of cold spit
– a whit
– diddly-squat
– one dog's cock
– the rind of a lemon
– three damns
– twopence/tuppence/four-pence ha'penny
– two tin fucks

FUN, HAVING *See* **JOYS OF LIFE**

FUNNY

funny …
– **as a bit of string** [1930s+]
– **as a box of worms** [20C] (N.Z.)
– **as a crutch** [1910s–60s] (US)
– **enough to give you a fit on the mat** [1900s–10s]
– **enough to make a cat laugh** [mid-19C+]
– **enough to make a dog laugh** [17C–early 19C]
funny peculiar or funny ha-ha? [1930s+] asking the speaker
   whether 'funny' means odd or amusing

G

GAY

See also EUPHEMISMS

Being Gay

behind with the rent [20C]

bent as a nine-bob note (also **bent as a forty-eight pence piece**) [1950s+]

b.o.b. [1990s+] (US prison) an effeminate male homosexual (i.e. '*b*end *o*ver *b*ackwards')

light in the loafers (also **light on her feet**) [1950s+] (US)

like that [1970s+] (UK)

hint of mint [1950s+] (US gay) a trace of homosexual tendencies

Queer as ...

– a clockwork orange [1950s+]

– a coot [1920s+]

– a three-dollar bill [20C]

– a three-pound note [20C]

– beer [20C] (Aus.)

three times as queer as a three-dollar bill [1960s+]
(hence the phr. nine-dollar bill, a homosexual)

on the down low (also on the d.l., on the low) [20C] (orig. US
Black) of a (married) man, having homosexual relations
despite parading an ostensibly heterosexual lifestyle

on the other bus [1990s]

A Gay Miscellany

be one of the knights [1940s–70s] to have syphilis

butch it up [20C] (of either sex) to pose as 'masculine'

deliver a baby [1960s+] (US) to expose one's erect penis

do the bird circuit [1950s+] (US) to visit a succession of bars
in order to ascertain the whereabouts of the most attractive
men

dongs and gongs [20C] (orig. US) the penis and testicles

draw the curtains [1980s+] (US) to fellate an uncircumcised
penis

Doing the Bird Circuit

go to Copenhagen/Denmark [1950s+] to have a sex-change operation (ref. to a pioneering operation in Denmark in 1952)

harvest the cherries [1920s+] to take a youth and deprive him of his virginity

have a dishonourable discharge [1960s+] to masturbate after failing to make a sexual connection

picking up the vibrations [1940s–70s] watching other men perform a sex show, all-male voyeurism

something's rotten in Denmark [1950s+] ref. to someone who is presumed to have had a sex change (from 'Something is rotten in the state of Denmark', *Hamlet* (1602) I. iv. 90)

take it! [1930s–60s] an excl. used by someone demanding fellatio

tell a French joke [1960s–70s] to stimulate the anus orally

vanilla sex [1980s+] a phr. for relatively conventional forms of sexual activity, usu. in contrast to sado-masochistic sex

Gay Banter

are you prepared? (also **are you ready?**) [1960s+] (orig. US gay) implying amazement or shock, both approving and disapproving

cottage crawl [1950s+] to frequent public lavatories for sex

French bathe [1950s+] to use perfumes as a deodorant in lieu of bathing

have a cup of tea [1960s+] to have sex in a public lavatory

hung like a doughnut [1960s+] (US) a woman, i.e. one who has a vagina (a hole)

Jewish by hospitalization [1950s+] circumcised but not Jewish

like a butterfly on heat [1970s] (orig. gay) dithering frantically

make a milk run [1990s] (US) to hang around a public lavatory looking for sex

mercy mary! [1950s+] an excl. of surprise

or days! [1950s+] an excl. implying shock or amazement

b.p.o.m. [1950s–70s] *b*ig *p*iece *o*f *m*eat

I.B.M. [1960s+] a small penis; i.e. '*i*tty *b*itty *m*eat'

n.a.f.f. [1980s] *n*ot *a*vailable *f*or *f*ucking/*f*un

o.m.c.d. [1960s+] *o*ut *o*f *m*y *c*lass *d*arling

s.y.t. [1950s+] (Aus.) *s*weet *y*oung *t*hing (of a boy or girl according to context)

t.b.h. [1980s+] a potential sexual conquest; i.e. '*t*o *b*e *h*ad'

---

pick up the soap for someone [1960s–70s] to allow oneself to be sodomized

play checkers [1960s+] move from seat to seat in a cinema in search of a receptive sex partner

plug in the neon [1960s+] (US) to have an orgasm

Princeton rub [1950s+] body-to-body rubbing

Ribena on toast [1980s+] said of someone who is unavailable for sex (from the unlikeliness of the dish)

Vaseline Villa [1960s+] a Y.M.C.A. frequented by gay men

HANGED, TO BE

See also BREAKFASTING

bless the world with one's heels [mid-16C–mid-17C]
catch the stifles [17C]
climb the ladder [16C+]
climb the leafless tree [early–mid-19C]
climb the stalk [18C]
cry cockles [late 18C]
cut a caper upon nothing (also **cut caper sauce**) [late 18C]
cut one's last fling [18C]
dangle in the sheriff's picture-frame [late 18C–early 19C]
die in a horse's nightcap [late 18C–mid-19C]
die in one's boots/with one's boots on [late 17C–1910s]
die like a dog (in a string) [late 17C–18C]

die on a fish day [late 17C–18C] (? because hangings took place on Catholic 'fish days', i.e Wednesdays and Fridays)

die the death of a trooper's horse [late 18C–early 19C]

go off with the fall of the leaf [late 18C–19C]

go to heaven in a string [late 16C–early 18C]

go up a tree [1910s+]

go upstairs out of the world [late 17C–early 18C]

go up the ladder to bed [late 16C–19C]

keep an ironmonger's shop by the side of a common [late 18C–early 19C] to be hanged in chains

kick before the hotel door [late 18C–mid-19C]

kick the clouds [late 18C–early 19C]

leap at a daisy [mid-16C–early 17C]

leap from the leafless tree [early–mid-19C]

leap up a ladder [17C–early 18C]

leave the world with cotton in one's ears [19C] (from the Rev. *Cotton*, who preached final sermons to the condemned at Newgate)

make a wry mouth [17C]

mount the cart [18C]

mount the ladder [16C–mid-19C]

nap the winder [mid-19C–1930s]

piss where one cannot whistle [late 18C–early 19C] (from the loss of bowel control that accompanies hanging)

preach on Tower Hill [16C] (a London place of execution)

ride the horse foaled of an acorn [mid-17C–mid-19C]

shake a cloth in the wind [late 18C–mid-19C] to be hanged in chains

sus. per coll. [late 18C–early 19C] (Lat. *suspensus per collum*, hanged by the neck; this was the notation entered in the prison ledger)

swing in a halter [mid–late 16C]

take a leap in the dark [17C–early 18C]

take the long jump [1920s–60s]

trine to the cheats [mid-16C–18C] (SE *trine*, march to the gallows; *cheats*, gallows)

To Die at Tyburn

Tyburn was formerly London's main place of execution, located where Marble Arch now stands. Its famous Triple Tree was a three-cornered gallows, capable of dispatching 21 persons at a time. Several expressions meaning 'to hang' refer to Tyburn and its Tree:

climb the triple tree [18C]

dangle in a Tyburn string [late 18C]

fetch a Tyburn stretch [16C]

leap at Tyburn [late 17C–early 19C]

make a Tyburn show [late 18C–early 19C]

preach at Tyburn cross [late 16C–18C]

take a leap at Tyburn [17C–early 19C]

Dangled on a Hempen Rope

choked by a hempen quinsey [late 18C–early 19C]

die of a hempen fever [18C–early 19C]

frisk in a hempen cravat [18C]

look through a hempen window [17C]

pull hemp [mid-19C–1950s] (US)

stabbed with a Bridport dagger [mid-17C–18C] (the best variety of British hemp was grown at Bridport, Dorset)

stretch (the) hemp [mid–late 19C]

wag hemp in the wind [mid-16C–early 17C]

walk up Ladder Lane and down Hemp Street [19C]

wear a hempen necktie [late 17C–18C]

Dancing in the Air

To be hanged is to **dance ...**

– **at Beilby's ball (where the sheriff plays the music/pays the fiddlers)** (also **shake one's trotters at Beilby's ball**) [late 18C] (the identity of Beilby has not been established)

– **at the sheriff's ball (and loll one's tongue out at the** company) [late 18C–early 19C]

– at Tuck 'em Fair [18C]

– on air [late 19C–1940s] (US)

– on/upon nothing (at the sheriff's door/in a hempen cravat) [late 18C]

– the Newgate hornpipe [late 18C–mid-19C]

– the Paddington frisk [late 17C–early 19C]

– the Tyburn hornpipe on nothing [late 18C–mid-19C]

– the Tyburn jig [late 17C–early 19C]

do the dance [1930s] (US)

do the Newgate frisk [19C]

HAPPY *See* **JOYS OF LIFE**

HARM, TROUBLE AND STRIFE

See also CRIME AND THE UNDERWORLD; DOO-DOO, TO BE IN DEEP; VIOLENT AND UNTIMELY END, TO BRING ABOUT A

all up the country with [late 19C–1930s] to be the ruin of, to be the death of

at sixes and sevens [late 19C+] (US) badly disturbed, upset

cruising for a bruising [1940s+] (orig. US) looking deliberately to cause or get into trouble

devil to pay and no pitch hot [early 18C–mid-19C] trouble in prospect or coming as a consequence

do dirt to someone (also **do someone dirt**, **do dirt by someone**) [late 19C+] to harm, to injure deliberately, often verbally

do oneself a naughty [1970s+] to injure oneself

fry/cook someone's bacon [late 19C+] to cause difficulties or unhappiness for someone else

he'd crap on a marble shit house [early 19C+] used of someone who causes trouble for its own sake

his hair grows through his hood [mid-15C–early 18C] used of someone considered to be 'on the road to ruin'

if it ain't you, it's somebody else [1930s+] (US Black) a phr. in which the speaker indicates a belief that trouble is imminent

I'll nark you [1910s+] (Aus.) I'll ruin your plan

play the deuce with [17C+] to cause trouble for, to incommode, to make a mess of

put a kick in someone's gallop [20C] (Ulster) to ruin someone's plans, to 'put a spoke in their wheel'

put a nail in someone's coffin [early 18C+] to cause trouble, to accelerate decline

put the bee/B on [1910s–40s] (US) to quash, to bring to an end, to ruin

put the fritz on (also **put the fritz to**, **put on the fritz**, **put on the fritzerine**) [20C] to spoil, to render out of order, to put a stop to

put the kibosh on [mid-19C+] to spoil, to ruin

raise Cain [mid-19C+] (orig. US) to cause as much trouble as one can

raise Ned [mid-19C+] to cause a disturbance, to make trouble

screwed, blued and tattooed (also **screwed, jewed and tattooed**) [1960s–70s] (US) comprehensively defeated; suffering very great harm

that's torn it [20C] that's spoiled one's chances, put an end to one's plans

that's your little red wagon [1930s–70s] (US Black) that's your problem

wouldn't bust a fart in a ghost-town [1990s] used of one who would never break the law or cause the least trouble

Assault and Battery

anoint with oil of hazel (also **anoint with oil of gladness**) [late 18C–19C] to beat (a variety of sap supposedly contained in a green hazel rod, which adds vigour to a beating)

beat/pound the stuffing out of [late 19C]

beat/kick/knock the bejazus/baby jesus/plazazus out of [mid-19C+]

beat/clean/kick/knock/whale the crap out of [late 19C+] (orig. US)

beat/knock the pants off [1920s+]

beat someone till his hide won't hold hay/shavings/shucks [20C] (US)

crawl someone's hump [19C+] (US) to attack, to assault

curry someone's skin-coat [18C–mid-19C] to thrash, to beat

dust someone's jacket /coat/linen/back (also **lace someone's jacket**) [late 17C–1910s]

give someone Larry Dooley [1940s+] (Aus.) to beat someone, to punish (after *Larry* Foley, late 19C Aus. boxer; the phr. began by using the proper name, but soon replaced Foley by Dooley)

knock all over the shop [mid–late 19C]

knock seven bells/kinds of hell out of [1920s+]

lace into [early 19C+] to attack, to beat, to thrash

put someone on the bum [late 19C+] (US) to hurt someone, to beat someone up

tan someone's hide/arse/jacket [late 17C+]

Beaten and Overwhelmingly Defeated

done like a dog's dinner [1930s+] (N.Z.)

run home on one's ear [late 19C] (US)

whipped like a dog [1980s+]

whipped out of one's boots [late 19C] (US)

whipped to a custard [late 19C] (US)

J K

JOYS OF LIFE, THE

far fucking out! [1960s+] a general expression of pleasure, delight, appreciation etc.

fine as frog hair [20C] (US) feeling very well or very cheerful

full of beans [mid-19C+] enthusiastic, excited, cheerful

home on the pig's back [1910s+] (Aus./N.Z.) very contented, happily or successfully placed, having arrived at a successful conclusion

hot puppy! [1920s+] (US) an excl. of pleasure

in a good /whole skin [late 18C–1910s] good-humoured, cheerful

in (full/high) feather [19C+] in top condition, very cheerful, rich

in high/great snuff [mid-19C–1930s] elated, very happy

in one's ackee/salt [1940s+] (W.I.) energetic, cheerful (*ackee*, a popular W.I. fruit, usu. accompanied by *salt*fish, and giving rise to cheerfulness)

in one's glory [late 19C] extremely happy and satisfied

in the pink [mid-18C+] extremely fit, well and cheerful

keep one's pecker up (also **hold one's pecker up**) [mid-19C+] to stay cheerful, despite possible adversity; 'never say die!; often **keep your pecker up!**

like a possum up a gum-tree [late 19C–1950s] (Aus.) absolutely content, perfectly happy

Home on the Pig's Back

like a flea in a honeymooner's bed [late 19C–1950s] (Aus.) as above

look like a kookaburra that has swallowed the kangaroo [1930s+] (Aus.) to look elated, to look very happy

max and relax [1980s+] (US Black/campus) to take life easy, to enjoy oneself; esp. in the phr. **maxin' and relaxin'**

on a high [1960s+] feeling very happy and positive

A Nun Weeding the Asparagus

- a black in a barrel of treacle [19C]
- a clam (at high tide/water) [mid-19C+] (US)
- a couple of cock canaries on a May morning [19C]
- a dog with two tails/a tin tail/two dicks [20C]
- a flea at a dog show [1990s+] (N.Z.)
- a nun weeding the asparagus [1910s+] (Can.) (with obvious sexual overtones given the 'phallic' asparagus)
- a pig in shit/clover/muck/mud [late 19C+]
- **Larry** [20C] (orig. Aus.) (poss. Larry *Foley* (1847–1917), Aus. boxer)

r. & i. [1980s+] (US campus) extremely exciting or enjoyable; i.e. 'radical and intense'

(riding) high, wide and handsome [20C] (orig. US) happy, pleasant, carefree, performing well and easily

stoke me! (also **stoke me up!**) [1980s+] (US campus) a general excl. of approval, that's wonderful! I'm so happy! great!

the most fun you can have with your pants on [20C] (Aus.)

this is the life [20C] (orig. US) a general excl. of happiness, enthusiasm, pleasure etc.

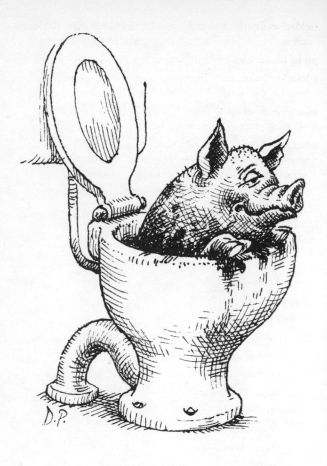

A Pig in Shit

tickled to death (also **tickled silly, tickled to bits, tickled to pieces**) [20C] delighted, very happy, amused

up in the air/sky [19C+] happy, in a good mood

whatever bakes your biscuit [1980s+] (US) whatever makes you happy, satisfied

whatever floats your boat [1980s+] (US) a general phr. of acquiescence: whatever you like

whatever turns you on [1970s+] whatever you like, esp. as slightly sarcastic response to a revelation of an especially bizarre or distasteful pleasure (usu. sexual)

Merry as ...

- **a cricket** [mid-16C+]
- **a Greek** [mid-16C–late 17C]
- **a cuckoo** [mid-19C+]
- **a grig** [mid-16C+]
- **a magpie** [late 14C–early 17C]
- **beggars** [mid-17C–mid-18C]
- **he that has nought to lose** [mid–late 17C]
- **mice in malt** [early 17C–late 19C]
- **the maids** [mid–late 17C]
- **three chips** [mid–late 16C]
- **wedding bells** (also **a marriage-bell**) [mid-19C+]

Keen as a Bean

all to the mustard (also **so much to the mustard**) [1900s–20s]
    (US)

full of piss and vinegar [1940s+] (orig. US)

going ahead like a whale [late 19C]

going bananas over something [1960s+] (orig. US)

hot-shit for … [1970s+] (US)

keen as a bean [20C] (Aus.)

with a hey nonny-nonny and a hotcha-cha [1930s+]
    (orig. US) an excl. of enthusiasm

young, dumb and full of cum [1970s+] (US) used of a
    teenager or young person whose enthusiasm for life
    (and esp. sex) outweighs their intelligence

KILLING *See* **VIOLENT AND UNTIMELY END,
TO BRING ABOUT A**

L

LAZY

do you feel like that? [late 19C] ironic phr. addressed to a
normally lazy person who is, for a change, working

he wouldn't work in an iron lung [1940s+] (Aus.)

lazy as a Maori dog [1950s] (N.Z.)

lazy as Joe the marine [19C] (from the proverb *as lazy as Joe
the marine, who laid his musket down to sneeze*)

lazy as Ludlam's dog. [mid-19C] (from the proverb *as lazy
as Ludlam's dog, which leaned its head against the wall to
bark*)

Lazy Lawrence [mid-18C–1900s] the embodiment of
laziness (from the story that the martyr St *Lawrence* refused
to make a sound as he was roasted to death, causing his
executioner to suggest that far from being stoic, he was
too lazy)

not do a tap (of work) [late 19C–1950s] to be absolutely idle

not exactly one of the world's workers [1930s+]

work at Idle Hall [20C] (W.I.) to be unemployed

LEAVE ME ALONE

See also ABUSE, MISCELLANEOUS; DISBELIEF, SURPRISE, ANNOYANCE; DISMISSAL AND CONTEMPT

away and claw mould on yourself [20C] (Ulster)

ax/axe my arse! [mid-18C+] a harshly negative response to what is considered an irrelevant or over-familiar question, i.e., go to hell! fuck off!

Make Like a ...

[1950s+] (US) ... part of a number of phrases all of which mean 'go away', 'get lost', thus, **make like a ...**

– banana and split

– cow pat and hit the trail

– dragster and lay rubber

– drum and beat it

– fart and blow away

– paper doll and cut out

– rubber and roll

– tree and leave

---

be missing! [1920s+] (US) (a phr. first used by Chicago mobster Spike O'Donnell in rejecting the overtures/threats of Al Capone (1899–1947), a rival)

blow yourself! [late 19C] (US)

butt out! [1960s+]

creep away and die! [1920s]

don't call us, we'll call you [1940s+]

eat shit! (and die!) [1930s+] (US)

get the fuck (out)! [1950s+]

kiss off! [1930s+]

mash dog! [20C] (W.I.) (from *mash*, a call to a dog, meaning go or walk)

oh swallow yourself! [late 19C]

paws off! [20C]

paws off, Pompey [early 19C–1930s] (coined *c.*1803 without the comma, as 'paws off Pompey' and used as an anti-Napoleonic phr., meaning 'keep your hands off Pompey' (a nickname either for Lord Nelson or the naval town of Portsmouth). By the 1830s the comma had been introduced and the phr. was generally used by women wishing to restrain an admirer's wandering hands)

pox take you! [late 16C+]

run away and play marbles! [late 19C+]

run away and play trains! [20C]

run away and play with yourself! [20C]

shape up or ship out [1950s+] (orig. milit.)

take a running jump (at the moon)! [20C]

Eating Pussy

you're as welcome as a fart in a phone box [20C] (Aus.)

zandoli your hole! [20C] (W.I.) (from *zondoli*, lizard, which moves fast and lives in holes in the ground)

Go ...

– **bark at the moon!** [1960s]

– **beat your meat!** [1930s+] (US)

– **bite the bag!** [1950s+] (US)

– **blow!** [late 19C+] (US)
– **crap in your hat (, pull it over your head and call it curls)** [1940s+] (US)
– **crawl up a hole!** [1940s+] (Aus.)
– **dip your eye in cocky's shit** [20C] (Aus.)
– **eat pussy!** [1950s+] (US Black)
– **fall on yourself!** [late 19C] (US)
– **frig youself!** [1930s–50s]
– **fuck a duck!** [20C]
– **fuck yourself!** [late 19C+]
– **jump in a lake!** [1910s+]
– **jump yourself!** [20C] (orig. US)
– **lay an egg!** [1930s] (US campus)
– **milk a duck!** [20C] (US campus) euph. for *go fuck a duck*!
– **peddle your fish!** [1930s] (US)
– **piss up a rope!** [20C] (orig. US)
– **roll your hoop!** [late 19C+] (US)
– **shit in a pot and duck your head** [1940s+] (US)
– **shit in your hat, pull it over your head and call it flowers** [1940s+] (US)
– **shit in your wallet** [1940s+] (US)
– **sit on a tack** [1930s] (US campus)
– **spit in your hat!** [1940s+] (US)
– **spit up your trouser leg** [1940s+] (US)
– **to blazes!** [mid-19C+]
– **to buggery!** [late 19C+]

Off with You!

bog off! [1950s+] (orig. RAF)

bugger off! [1920s+] (abbr. to **b.o.** in the 1950s)

fuck off! [1920s+] (abbr. to **f. off!** in the 1940s)

sod off! [20C]

step off! [1990s] (US Black teen)

– **to father!** [late 19C–1900s] euph. for *go to hell!*

– **to France** [20C] (W.I.) euph. for *go to hell!*

– **to grass (and eat hay)!** [19C+] (US)

– **to Hanover!** [18C] (alluding to the contemporary dislike of the Hanoverian monarchs)

– **to hell!** [mid-18C+]

– **to hell and pump thunder!** [late 19C]

– **to hell, Hull and Halifax!** [16C+]

– **to hell or Connaught!** [mid-17C–late 19C]

– **to pot!** [mid-19C+]

– **to the billy-fencer and sell yourself for bull-beef** [mid-19C]

Go and ...
– **boil your head!** [1930s+]

– **bust yourself!** [mid-19C+]

– **eat coke!** [late 19C+]

– **fry your face!** [late 19C–1900s]

– **fuck yourself!** [mid-19C+]

– **get cut!** [20C] (Aus.)

– **piss up a shutter!** [1910s+]

– **play trains with yourself!** [20C]

– **scrape yourself!** [late 19C]

– **take a run against the wind!** [20C] (Anglo-Irish)

– **take a running jump at yourself** [20C]

LOVE *See* **SEX, MOSTLY**

LYING, CHEATING AND DOWNRIGHT DECEIVING

To Trick and Swindle

build pigpens [20C] (US) to deceive, esp. of a merchant who cheats a customer

come yankee over (also **come yankee with/play yankee over/ play yankee with**) [mid-19C+]

double-bank [late 19C–1940s] (US)

give it to (someone) on the billiard slum [early 19C–1910s] (Aus.)

have (someone) on a string [mid-19C–1930s]

lay the note [1920s–70s] (US underworld)

lie like a flatfish [1960s] to lie skilfully and continually

lie like a pig [20C] (Aus.) to tell plausible lies

pull a shrewdy [20C] (Aus./N.Z.)

pull a swiftie [1940s+] (Aus./N.Z.)

put game on someone [1950s+] (US Black)

put in the cart [late 19C+]

put one over (on) (also **slip one over**, **put something over on**, **sneak one over on**) [late 19C+] (orig. US)

run a blazer (US) [mid–late 19C]

sell someone a packet [late 19C]

stun out of [mid-19C] (UK underworld)

suck out of the thumb [20C] (S.Afr.) to lie, to make up, to fabricate

swing it on across [20C] (mainly Aus./N.Z.)

throw the hooks into (US) [late 19C–1940s]

Dishonest and Illegal

bent as a nine-bob note (also **bent as a forty-eight pence piece**) [1950s+]

on the beat [late 19C–1900s] (US) engaged in a swindle

on the bugle [1940s] (Aus.)

on the crook (also **on the crooked**) [15C–late 19C]

on the cross [early 19C+]

on the dodge [20C]

on the lay [18C–1900s]

on the sharp [mid-19C] attempting to defraud victims

out of the straight [late 19C+]

Smelling a Rat

come, come, that's Barney Castle [late 19C] a response given to someone making a specious excuse (from the Rising of the North by the Catholic earls in 1569, when Sir George Bowes refused, despite many opportunities, to leave his fortified position in Barnard Castle to engage in battle)

dead cat up the branch [20C]

dead duck up the stream [20C]

don't come the old abdabs (also **don't give me the abdabs**) [1940s]

don't hang dirty washing in my backyard [1940s] (US Black)

don't piss on my back and tell me it's raining [20C] (Aus.)

don't play the traveller [late 18C–19C]

lame as St Giles Cripplegate [17C–19C] of a lie, very 'lame' indeed (*St Giles* is the patron saint of cripples)

out of whole cloth [mid–late 19C] (US) used of a statement that is a blatant lie, usu. with the verbs *make...*, *manufacture...*, *cut...*

there's a dead nigger in the woodpile [20C] (US)

MAD

See also DAZED AND CONFUSED; STUPID

a button short [19C+]

all over the board [1960s–1970s]

another one for the van [1920s+] implying that the person
should be collected by the van going to a psychiatric
institution; hence the 1950s joc. cry **send for the
green van!**

apartments to let [mid-19C+]

around/round the twist/bend [20C]

as odd as God's off-ox [19C+] (US) (from SE *off-ox*, the
ox harnessed to the *offside* of the team)

barmy as a bandicoot [1950s+] (N.Z.)

cracked in the filbert [late 19C–1920s]

crazy as a bedbug [1920s+] (orig. US)

dicked in the nob [early–mid-19C]

from outer space [1950s+] (US)

gone off one's dip [late 19C–1910s]

have a canary [1960s+] (US)

have a few of one's pages stuck together [20C]

have a tile loose [mid-19C]

have bugs (in the head) (also **have bugs in one's head**) [20C] (orig. US)

his head is not sweet [20C] (W.I.)

lightly sprung [1980s+]

like a monkey on a stick [late 19C+]

little bit off the top [1910s+] (Aus.)

lost a button [19C+]

not wrapped too tight [1970s+] (US)

off the hooks [17C–late 19C]

out of town [1940s–1960s] (US)

queer in the attic/garret [19C]

rats in the attic [20C]

row with one oar [20C] (US)

soft in the head [late 18C+]

two stops on from Dagenham [20C] (the station in question is Barking, as in 'barking mad')

up the pole [late 19C+]

up the stick [1930s+]

up the wall [1920s+] (US)

Mad as ...

– **a beetle** [1910s+] (Aus.)

– **a Chinaman** [1910s+] (Aus.)

– **a dingbat** [1910s+] (Aus.)

– **a goanna** [1910s+] (Aus.)

– **a gum-tree full of galahs** [1910s+] (Aus.)

– **a (March) hare** [14C–15C+] (alluding to the hare's sexual excitement, which peaks in March)

– **a hatter** [mid-19C] (alluding to the use in the 18C of mercurous nitrate in the tanning of felt hats. This was absorbed by the hatters, in whom the effects could produce mental problems)

– **a hornet** [1910s+] (Aus.)

– **a maggot** [20C] (N.Z.)

– **May butter** [17C] (the warmth of May makes the making of butter especially difficult)

– **a meat axe** [1920s+] (Aus./ N.Z.)

– **mud** [1920s]

– **snakes** [1910s+] (Aus.)

– **tucker** [1910s+] (Aus.)

– **a weaver** [17C] (proverbial wisdom associates insanity with weavers)

One Sausage Short of a B.B.Q. ...

couple of bottles short of a six-pack [1980s+]

couple of chips short of a fish dinner [20C]

couple of tinnies short of a slab [1980s+]

few bricks short of a load [1960s+]

few pence short in the shilling [1900–60s]

few spring rolls short of a banquet [20C]

five annas short of the rupee [19C+]

no more than ninepence in the shilling [late 19C]

not have all one's buttons [mid–late 19C]

not have both oars in the water [20C]

not play with a full deck [1960s+]

not the full cup of tea [1970s+]

not the full dollar [1970s+] (Aus.)

not the full quid [1970s+] (Aus./N.Z.)

not the full shilling [20C]

one sandwich short of the picnic [1960s+]

one sausage short of a B.B.Q. [1990s] (US teen)

only 80 pence in the pound [20C]

only one and ninepence in the florin/two shillings/two bob
   [1910–70s]

tenpence short of the full quid [mid–19C]

two wafers short of a communion [1960s+]

MASTURBATION: ONAN'S OLYMPICS

[19C] [the biblical *Onan*, who 'cast his seed upon the ground'
(Genesis 38:9)

The Act of Onan: Pulling One's Plonker

address congress [1990s] (US)

adjust one's set [1980s+]

apply the hand brake [1980s+]

appropriate the means [1980s+]

audition the finger puppets [1980s+]

be your own best friend [1990s]

bequeath one's genes [1990s]

bleed the weed [1990s]

bloat the vein [1990s]

blow one's dust [1960s–70s]

blow one's own horn [1990s]

buck the bone [1990s]

burp the baby [1990s]

chafe at the bit [1990s]

charge the rod [1990s]

check one's oil [1930s+] (US)

chong your schlong [1990s]

clamp the pipe [1990s]

clean one's rifle [20C]

climb the tree [20C]

clobber the Kleenex [1990s]

close the deal [1990s]

cock one's shotgun [1990s]

come into your own [1980s+]

come to grips with yourself [1990s]

consult Dr Jerkoff [20C] (US)

converse with Harry Palm [1990s] (perhaps a ref. to the hairs that supposedly grow on a masturbator's palm, plus possibly a ref. to Len Deighton's anonymous intelligence agent anti-hero, named Harry Palmer for the films (1960s) starring Michael Caine)

crank one's/the shank [20C]

create an arch [1990s]

crimp the wire [1990s]

cruise for an oozing [1990s]

To Get ...

- **a grip on things** [1990s]
- **comfortable** [1990s]
- **in touch with one's inner-self** [1990s]
- **one's pole varnished** [1980s+]
- **one's rocks off** [1960s+]
- **the dirty water off one's chest** [20C]
- **to know yourself** [1990s]

---

dash one's doodle [19C]

date Rosy Palm and her sisters/five sisters [20C]

defrost the fridge [1990s]

diddle the dinky [1980s+]

diddy ride [1990s]

dig for change [1900s]

dinky one's slinky [1960s+]

To Make ...

– **a foreskin cone** [1990s]

– **a rendezvous with Mrs Hand** [1980s+]

– **a six-fist** [1990s]

– **a solo flight** [1990s]

– **fist-kabobs** [1990s]

– **friends with Big Ed** [1990s]

– **instant pudding** [1990s]

– **out with yourself** [1950s+] (US)

– **prick juice** [1990s]

– **soup** [1990s]

– **the bald man puke/sick** [1990s]

– **the hooded cobra spit** [1990s]

– **the rooster crow** [1990s]

– **the scene with the magazine** [1900s]

To Polish ...

– and gloss [20C]
– Charlie Brown [1980s+]
– one's antlers [1980s+]
– one's knob [1980s+]
– one's sword [1980s+]
– percy [1980s+]
– the lighthouse [1980s+]
– the penguin [1980s+]
– the pole [1980s+]
– the rocket [1980s+]
– the sword [1980s+]
– the viper [1980s+]

download one's floppy [1990s]
drain Charles Dickens [1990s]
drive the skin bus [1990s]
dust the end-table [1990s]
dust the family jewels [1990s]
empty the cannon [1980s+]
engage in safe sex [1980s+]
examine the equipment [1990s]
express yourself [1980s+]

feel in one's pocket for one's big hairy rocket [20C]

fetch mettle [17C–early 19C]

fight the champ [1980s+]

file one's fun-rod [20C]

fire one's peter [20C]

fire the flesh musket [20C]

fire the hand cannon [20C]

fire the wobbly warhead [1980s+]

firk the dude [20C]

fist fuck [1960s+]

fist one's mister [20C]

free the slaves [1990s]

friendly fire [1980s+]

To Have ...

– **a ball** [1940s+] (orig. US)

– **a conversation with the one-eyed trouser snake** [1960s+]

– **a taffy pulling contest** [20C] (US)

– **a tug o' war with ol' cyclops** [1990s]

– **a whack attack** [1970s+]

– **an arm wrestle with your one-eyed vessel** [1990s]

– **the urge for a surge** [1990s]

A Conversation with the One-Eyed Trouser Snake

fuck Mrs Palmer [1990s]

fuck one's fist [20C]

fuck Palmela [1990s] (play on 'palm')

fuck without complications [1990s]

gallop one's/the antelope [mid-19C+]

give it a tug [1950s+]

give yourself a low five [1980s+]

give Yul Brynner a high five [1990s] (ref. to the bald-headed
  Hollywood actor)

glue the lady's eyes shut [1990s]

go blind [20C]

go mingo [mid-19C]

go on a date with Handrea and Palmela [1990s]

go on peewee's little adventure [1980s] (US)

go steady with one's right hand [1970s+] (US)

gob and rub [1960s]

grab the flab/slab [1990s]

grease one's pipe [20C]

grease one's pole [1990s]

grip the gold [1990s]

grip the pencil [1990s]

grip the tip [1990s]

hack one's mack [20C]

hand shandy [20C]

hang the old man [20C]

haul one's own ashes [20C] (US)

hit on Rosy Palm [20C]

hitchhike under the big top [1990s]

hold one's own [20C]

hold the bold [1990s]

hump one's hose [20C]

ignite the lightsaber [1980s+] (ref. to weapon in *Star Wars* films)

iron some wrinkles [1990s]

keep down the census [19C]

kill it [1990s]

knock on wood [20C]

knock one out [1990s]
knock one's own thing [20C] (W.I./Belize)
lather a bar of soap [1920s–50s] (US)
let loose the juice [1990s]
lick the dick [1980s+]
lighten the load [1980s+]
load/man the cannon [1980s+]
man the cockpit [1980s+]
massage the one-eyed monk [1990s]
meet Mary Palm and her five sisters [1950s+]
meet Rosie Hancock [1950s+]
meet with Mother Thumb and her daughters [20C]
meet your right-hand man [1990s]
mind one's own business [1990s]
mount a corporal and four [late 18C–early 19C]
negotiate a new contract [1990s]
oil the glove [1990s]
organize the family jewels [1990s]
pack one's palm [1990s]
paint the ceiling [1990s]
pan for white gold [1990s]
pass math [1990s] (US)
perform a self-test [1980s+]
please one's pisser [20C]
pocket the rocket [1990s]
pop a wad (by hand) [20C]

Massaging the One-Eyed Monk

pop one's cork [1960s+]

pop one's peter [1990s]

practise the Heimlich manoeuvre [1990s]

prime one's pump [1950s+]

prompt one's porpoise [20C]

prune the fifth limb [19C]

pump a gusher [1990s]

pump gas at the self-service island [1990s]

qualify in the testicular time trial [1990s]

rattle the bottle [1950s+] (US)

ride the great white knuckler [1990s]

ride the handcar [1940s+] (US)

rob the knob [1990s]

roll one's marbles [1950s] (US)

roll your own [1990s]

rub it up the wrong way [1990s]

rub the rod [20C]

rub up [mid-17C]

run off a batch by hand [1990s]

run one's hand up the flagpole [20C]

salute the sailor [1990s]

sand the banister/wood [1990s]

sap one's woody [1990s]

scrape/cut one's horns [1960s+] (US)

shake hands with Abraham Lincoln [1990s]

shake hands with the unemployed [1990s]

shake hands with the wife's best friend [1960s+]
shake the weasel [1990s]
shake up [19C]
shift gears [1990s]
shine one's pole [20C]
shine the barrel [1990s]
shine the helmet [1990s]
shoot for the moon [1990s]
shoot one's squirt [1990s]
shoot skeet [1990s]
shower spank [1980s+] (US teen)

To Take ...

– **a beating** [1960s+]
– **a load off one's mind** [1990s]
– **a shake break** [1990s]
– **an outing with Tom thumb and his four brothers** [20C]
– **matters into one's own hands** [20C]
– **one off the wrist** [1960s+]
– **one's snake for a gallop** [20C]
– **oneself in hand** [1950s+]
– **the monster for a one-armed ride** [1990s]

shuffle the deck [1990s]
single dingles [1990s]
siphon off the tank [1990s]
slap it [20C]
slap pappy [1990s]
slick one's stick [1990s]
slide the shaft [1990s]
slop out [1990s]
snap the rubber [1990s]
spin one's own propeller [1960s+] (US)
spin the record [1990s]
spit-polish the purple helmet [1990s]
spray the spectators [1990s]
spuff up [1990s]
stoke the furnace [1990s]
strain the main vein [1950s+]
strike the pink match [1960s+]
stroke one's oar [1970s] (US)
summon the genie [1990s]
talk quietly to oneself [1990s]
test one's batteries [1990s]
throw out [1990s]
tickle one's dick/fancy/pickle [20C]
touch oneself up [20C]
trim one's horn [1990s]
trim one's wick [1990s]

unclog the drain/pipes [20C]

unload the gun [1990s]

wake the dead [1990s]

walk old one-eye [1990s]

wank the crank [1960s+]

wanker the anchor [1990s]

watch the eyelid movies [1960s+]

wave the magic wand [1990s]

wax the buick [20C]

wax the car/surfboard [20C]

whip and top [20C]

whittle the stick [20C]

whiz jizzum [20C]

wrestle the bald-headed champion [1990s]

yang one's wang [20C]

yank one's crank [20C] (US)

yank one's wank [20C]

yank the plank [1990s]

yankee one's wankee [20C]

yuck your choad [1960s+]

A Bestiary of Beastliness

belt one's hog [20C] (US)

bleed the lizard [1990s]

burp the worm [1990s]

charm the serpent/snake [1990s]

choke the chicken/chook [20C]

choke the gopher [1970s+] (US)

come one's mutton/turkey [late 19C+]

corral the tadpoles [1990s]

crank the monkey [1990s]

cream one's beef/cock [1990s]

cuff the dragon [1990s]

decongest the weasel [1990s]

drain the monster [1980s+]

feed the ducks [1990s] (US)

fight one's turkey [20C]

fish for zipper trout [1990s]

free willy [1990s] (play on the 1993 movie title, *Willy*
  being a killer whale)

gallop the old lizard [20C]

grapple the gorilla [1980s+]

hack the hog [20C]

hug the hog [1990s]

launch the tadpoles [1990s]

lift the lizard [1990s]

log the dog/hog [1990s]

lope the mule/pony [1930s+] (US)

mess with moby [1990s] (*Moby Dick*, the eponymous great
  white sperm whale of Herman Melville's classic 1851 novel)

milk the chicken/chook [20C]

milk the lizard/maggot/moose [late 19C+]

molest the mole [1980s+]

pet the lizard [1970s+]

pluck one's chicken [1990s]

puff the one-eyed dragon [1960s+]

pump the monkey/python [1990s]

quiet the trouser snake [1990s]

ride the bull [1990s]

ride the dolphin [1920s+]

rope the goat/pony [1990s]

shemp the hog [1990s]

shoot (the) tadpoles [20C]

skin the goose [1970s] (US)

slay the one-eyed monster [1980s+]

sperm the worm [1990s]

stifle the stoat [1990s]

strangle the goose [1990s]

stroke/swing the (finless) dolphin [1920s+]

tame the beef weasel [1990s]

teach one's dog to spit [1990s]

tease one's crabs/the weasel [1990s]

torment the trouser trout [1990s]

torture the tentacle [1990s]

tug one's slug [1990s]

walk the dog [20C]

wax the dolphin [20C]

whack/wack the one-eyed worm/weasel [1960s+]

Strangling the Goose

Conking Cardinals and Crowning Kings

bang/bash/flip/murder the bishop [late 19C+]

bash/pummel the priest [1990s]

batter/buff/capture the bishop [1980s+]

box the Jesuit and get cockroaches [late 16C–early 19C]

conk the cardinal [late 19C+]

crown the king [1990s]

disobey/please/punish/rope the pope [1980s+]

flay the emperor [1990s]

Dirty Dancing

dance with johnnie one-eye [1980s+]

do a dry waltz with oneself [1940s+]

do the bachelor's shuffle [1980s+]

do the crazy hand jive [1960s]

do the pork sword jiggle [1990s]

do the solitary rhumba [1990s]

Food and Drink and Self-Abuse

accost/oscillate the Oscar Meyer [1980s+] (*Oscar Meyer*, a
popular US brand of wiener)

adjust the bowl of fruit [1980s+]

beef-stroke-it-off [1990s] (play on 'beef stroganoff')

bop/bob one's baloney [1970s+]

buff the banana [1980s+]

bust a nut [1990s]

butter one's corn [20C]

butter the muffin [1990s]

cheese off [1990s]

churn butter/man cream [20C]

clear the custard [1990s]

cream one's corn/the cheese/the pie [1990s]

cuddle the kielbasa [1990s] (*kielbasa*, a variety of Polish
  garlic sausage)

cuff the carrot [1990s]

frost the pastries [1990s]

hold the mayo [1990s]

hold the sausage hostage [1990s]

hone the cone [1990s]

kebab one's fist [1990s]

knead one's dough [1990s]

knead one's knockwurst [1990s]

knuckle the bone [1990s]

manipulate the mango [1990s]

massage the frankfurter [1950s] (Aus.)

master bacon [1990s]

milk one's dick/doodle/oneself [late 19C+]

paddle/paint the pickle [1990s]

peel some chillies [1990s]

peel the banana/carrot [1990s]

pip the pumpkin [1990s]

pop a nut [1960s+]

pump cream [1990s]

pump one's pickle [20C]

ram the ham [1990s]

roll the dough [1990s]

sample the secret sauce [1990s]

shake the bottle [1990s]

shell the bean pod [1990s]

shine the salami [1990s]

shuck the corn [20C]

slake the bacon [1990s]

slam/slap the ham/salami/salmon/spam [1950s+]

sling one's juice [19C]

squeeze the cheese [1990s]

stir one's stew/the batter [1950s+]

tease the weenie/wienie [1990s] (US)

toss the ham javelin [1990s]

tweak one's twinkie [20C]

wash the meat [20C]

yank the yam [20C]

Hitting Willie

bash the candle [1990s]

bash the stick [1950s+] (Aus.)

battle the purple-helmeted warrior [1980s+]

beat ...

– off [1960s+] (US)

– **one's dummy** [1970s+]

– **one's hog** [1970s+]

– **one's little brother** [1960s+]

– **one's meat** [late 19C+] (orig. US)

– **pete** [1980s+]

– **the bald-headed bandit** [1960s+]

– **the bishop** [1960s+] (orig. US)

– **the bologna** [20C]

– **the butter** [1990s]

– **the daisy** [1950s+]

– **the dog** [1930s+]

– **the pup** [1950s] (US)

– **the stick** [1990s]

belt it [1970s]

belt one's batter [1900s–40s]

biff off [1990s]

blast a pocket rocket [1990s]

boff/bounce one's boner [1990s]

bop one's richard [1990s]

box the bald champ/bozack/clown [1990s]

box with Richard [1990s] (i.e. 'dick')

buff one's helmet/the happy lamp/the wood [1980s+]

bugger one's hand [1990s]

bludgeon the beefsteak [1980s+]

choke Kojak [1990s] (*Kojak*, fictional US detective in an eponymous TV series, starring the bald Telly Savalas)

crack the bat/off a batch [1990s]

cuff one's dummy [1970s+]

flick the dick [1990s]

flog ...

– **one's dong** [20C]

– **one's donkey** [late 19C+]

– **one's dumber brother** [20C]

– **one's dummy** [1970s+]

– **one's mutton** [late 19C+]

– **the bishop** [late 19C+]

– **the daisy** [1950s+]

– **the dog** [20C]

– **the (finless) dolphin** [1920s+]

– **the hog** [20C]

– **the infidel** [20C]

– **the log** [1950s+]

flub the dub [20C] (US)

go a couple rounds with the ol' josh/champ [20C]

kill some babies [20C] (US)

mangle the midget [1990s]

plunk one's twanger [1990s]

pound ...

– **off** [1980s+] (US gay)

– **one's flounder** [1990s]

– **one's meat** [1950s+]

– **one's peenie** [1960s]

– one's pork [1960s]
– one's pud [1960s]
– the bald-headed moose [1990s]
– the pelican [1990s]
pummel the love truncheon [1990s]
punch the clown [1990s]
punish percy in the palm [1990s]
rough up the suspect [1990s]
slam the hammer/wapper [1990s]
slog the log [1970s+]
snap the whip [1990s]
thump one's pumper [20C]
twang one's/the wire [1950s+]
twist one's crank [20C]
whack/wack it [1960s+]
whack/wack willy [20C]
whip ...
– it [20C]
– off [20C] (US campus)
– one's dripper [1990s]
– one's dummy [1970s+]
– one's lizard [1970s+]
– one's wire [1970s+] (US campus)
– the baloney pony [1990s]
– the dummy [1990s]
– the pony [1990s]

– the weasel [1990s]

– up some sour cream [1990s]

wonk one's conker [20C]

J. Arthur Rhyming Slang

On 'wank':

bang the plank [1990s]

have a ham shank [20C]

have a Sherman [1980s+] (i.e. *Sherman* tank)

J. Arthur [1940s+] (i.e. *J. Arthur* Rank (1888–1972),
  cinema magnate)

Levy and Frank [20C] (London restaurateurs)

pull rank [20C]

Shabba [1990s] (i.e. reggae star *Shabba* Ranks)

shank [20C]

taxi-rank [1970s]

On 'strop':

whip and top [20C]

On 'toss':

polish and gloss [20C]

Making Sweet Music with Oneself

do a bathroom guitar solo [1990s]

hump the horn [20C]

kick the gong around [20C] (US)

play …

– a flute solo on one's meat whistle [20C]

– a lute solo [19C]

– a one-stringed guitar [1990s]

– a tune on the one-holed flute [19C+]

– an organ solo [1990s]

– chopsticks [1960s+]

– the skin flute [20C]

ring one's dong [1990s]

sing with Rosie [1990s]

strum the banjo [1990s]

tickle the ivory [1980s]

tootle one's flute [1980s+]

Worldwide Wanking

bomb the German helmet [1990s]

climb Mount Baldy [1990s]

do the Portuguese pump [1990s]

erupt Vesuvius [1990s]

get the German soldier marching [1980s+]

go to/come from Bangkok [1990s]

hitchhike to heaven [1990s]

part the Red Sea [1990s] (female masturbation)

turn Japanese [1990s] (from the supposed narrowing in ecstasy of the masturbator's eyes)

visit Niagara Falls [20C]

Double-Clicking One's Mouse: Female Masturbation

apply lip gloss [1980s+]

baste the tuna [1980s+]

beat the beaver [1970s+]

brush the beaver [1990s]

bury the knuckle [1990s]

catch a buzz [1970s+]

clap one's clit [1970s+]

clean one's fur coat [1990s]

clout one's cookie [1970s] (US)

club the clam [1960s+]

cook cucumbers [1960s+] (from the presumed use
 of a *cucumber* as a dildo)

do something for my chapped lips [1980s+]

do the two-finger slot rumba [1990s]

do the two-fingered shuffle [1990s]

drill for oil [1940s] (orig. US Black)

finger fuck [late 18C+]

finger pie [1950s+]

flick the bean [1990s]

floss the cat [1990s]

fondle the fig [1990s]

glaze the donut [1990s]

grease the gash [20C]

hit the slit [20C]

hose one's hole [20C]

hula-hoop [1990s]

itch the ditch [1990s]

lick one's lips [1990s]

light the candle [1990s]

lube the tube [1990s]

make waves (for the man in the boat) [1990s]

perm one's poodle [1990s]

pet the/one's poodle [1960s+]

play stinky pinky [20C]

play the beaver [1990s]

play with the little man in the boat [20C]

poke one's pussy [1960s+]

poke the pucker [1990s]

preheat the oven [1990s]

ride the waterslide [1990s]

scratch the itch/patch [1990s]

slam the clam [1960s+]

sling one's jelly [19C]

stir it up [1950s+]

stump-jump [20C]

take a dip [1990s]

tickle one's crack [19C]

wax the candle-stick [20C]

wax the womb [20C]

work in the garden [1990s]

MATRIMONY

See also SEX, MOSTLY

agree like cat and dog [late 17C] of a married couple, to fight continually

all-and-all [20C] (US) one's wife

another good man gone [19C+] used by male friends on the announcement of a man's engagement to be married

arrested by the white serjeant [late 18C–late 19C] said of a man who has been fetched out of the tavern by his wife

Barkis is willing [late 19C] indicating one's general willingness to do something; usu. in the context of a man accepting the necessity of marriage (the phr. coined in the novel *David Copperfield* (1850) by Charles Dickens)

dance in the hog trough [20C] **1** for an older sister to be left unmarried when a younger sibling has found a husband; occas. also used of boys. **2** to be the last child in a family to be married

do you think I'm made of money? [20C] admonishing someone, usu. a wife or child, who is spending the bread-winner's hard-earned cash with excessive abandon

give the mitt/hand [late 19C–1940s] (US) to reject, esp. in the context of a proposal of marriage

gone to visit his uncle [late 18C–19C] of a man who has deserted his wife soon after the marriage

grass widow [16C–19C] (orig. Anglo-Ind.) a woman whose husband is temporarily absent (from the phr. out to *grass*)

jump the broomstick [17C+] to enter into a common-law marriage; no civil or religious ceremony is undertaken, but the couple 'make their vows' by jumping over a broomstick or other obstacles/implements

live at the sign of the Queen's Head/in Queen Street, [late 18C–mid-19C] of a man, to be dominated by one's wife

living with mother now [late 19C] used by women to reject offers of marriage or of an affair

l.t.r. [1970s+] a *living together relationship*; i.e. marriage in all but the legalities

off the hook [1920s+] (Aus.) of a married man, out for a night with male friends only

on one's promotion [mid-19C] behaving in a way that indicates that not only is marriage on one's mind, but feasible as well

on the carpet [late 19C+] (US) of someone who is eager to marry, esp. a widow or widower

on the cull list [19C] (US) of a woman, unmarried and worried about it

on the market [late 19C+] of a girl, available for marriage

on the shelf [mid-19C+] of a woman (occas. a man), unmarried and worried about it, feeling that she has been 'put to one side'

put the bee on [1910s–30s] of a woman, to pursue a man with the intention of marriage. (from the SE phr. *have a bee in one's bonnet*)

retired to stud [1940s+] (Aus.) used of a woman who has abandoned social life for marriage

sister of the Charterhouse [early–mid-16C] a vociferous woman, esp. when arguing with her husband (ref. to the silent monks of the Charterhouse, who would be unable to answer back)

split the blanket [20C] (US) get divorced

take the number off the door [late 19C] used of a house where the wife is seen as stronger than her husband

tied to a woman's apron-strings [18C+] dominated by one's wife, or mother

why buy a cow when milk is so cheap? [1930s+] (US) why get married when sexually permissive women are so available?

MEAN *See* **MISERLY**

MENSTRUATION

On the Rag: Menstruating

all white and spiteful [20C]

at number one London [19C]

Aunt Minnie/Aunt Flo is visiting [20C]

back in the saddle (again) [1950s+] (US)

captain is at home [late 18C–mid-19C]

cardinal is come [late 18C–mid-19C]

caught a rat [1990s]

flag is up/danger signal is up [late 19C+] (US)

flying baker [20C]

gal's at the stockyards [20C] (US)

George called [20C] (Aus./US)

granny's coming [20C] (Aus./US)

it looks like a wet weekend [20C] (orig. Aus.)

it's wallflower week [20C]

Kit has come [late 19C+]

Mickey Mouse is kaput [1930s–40s] (US) sex is impossible
  because of menstruation

my little friend has come [1920s+] (orig. Can./Aus.)

my red-headed aunt has arrived [20C]

on the blob [1990s] (US)

on the rag [1930s+]

Red Sea is out [20C]

road making/road up for repairs [mid–late 19C]

the gator bit [20C] (US)

there's a letter in the post office [mid-19C+] (US)

Flash the Red Rag: To Menstruate

come around [20C] (US)

come crook [1950s] (Aus.)

come sick [20C] (US)

cover the waterfront [20C] (US)

The Menstrual Woman

bloody mary [1960s+] (US)

p.m.s. monster [1980s+] (US campus)
  (*pre-menstrual stress*)

red dog on a white horse [1970s+] (US Black)

entertain the general [20C] (US)

fall off the roof [1960s+]

flash the red rag [early 19C–1900s]

fly a flag [20C] (US)

fly the flag [mid-19C]

fly the red flag [20C]

have a little visitor [1920s+]

have a friend/have friends to stay [20C] (US Black)

have red sails in the sunset [20C]

have the buns on [20C] (Aus.)

have the decorators in [mid-19C+]

have the flag out [20C]

have the monkeys (also **her monkey's sick; her monkey's got a haemorrhage**) [1950s–60s] (US)

have the painters in [mid-19C+]

have the rag on [1950s+]

The Secret Language of Menstruation

d.a.s. *n.* [mid-19C–1920s] the menstrual flow; *d*omestic *a*fflictions

o.t.r. [1960s+] (US campus) i.e. '*o*n *t*he *r*ag'

p.m.s. [1990s] (US campus) of a woman, to feel irritable, anxious; *p*re-*m*enstrual *s*yndrome, or *p*utting up with *m*en's *s*hit

---

Surfing the Crimson Wave

put one's flags out [20C]
ride a cotton/white horse [20C]
ride the rag [1940s+]
stub one's toe [20C]
surf the crimson wave [1980s+] (US teen)

MISERLY

as full of gifts as a brazen horse of farts [late 18C]

he would skin a turd [late 19C+] (Can.)

mean as a louse [late 19C]

mean as dirt (also **meaner than dirt, mean as mud, mean as dish-water, meaner than goose grease**) [19C+] (US)

mean as garbroth [20C] (US) (*garbroth*, broth made from the garfish, generally seen as the food of the very poorest and as such not fit for human consumption)

Scotch as the devil [mid-19C]

so mean he'd lick the bowl when he's finished, rather than pull the chain [20C] (Aus.)

So Mean He Wouldn't ...

[20C] (Aus.)

– give a dog a drink at his mirage

– give a rat a railway pie

– give a shout if a shark bit him

– give a wave if he owned the ocean

– give you a fright if he was a ghost

– give you a light for your pipe at a bushfire

– give you a shock if he owned the powerhouse

– spit in your mouth if your throat was on fire

– give you his cold

Tight As ...

– a crab's/cow's arse [1960s]
– a fish's/duck's/flea's arsehole [20C]
– a gnat's twat [2000s]
– Kelsey's nuts [20C] (US) very mean, stingy
   (punning ref. to the US *Kelsey* Wheel Company,
   founded in 1910 to produce automobile wheels.
   The need for nuts and bolts to be exceptionally
   tight fitting to preclude wobbly wheels gave rise to
   the saying)
– O'Reilley's balls [20C] (US)

so mean he still has his lunch money from school [20C]
   (Aus.)
so mean he wouldn't give you the time of day [mid-19C+]
throw money around like a man with no hands [1940s]
   (Aus.)
tighter than a tick [20C] (Can.)
too mean to part with his own shit [20C] (US)

Tight as a Cow's Arse

MONEY

Filthy Lucre

bit of the old [mid-19C–1900s] money (usu. owed from gambling)

corn in Egypt [19C] money (from the phr. *corn in Egypt*, a plentiful supply, from Genesis 42:2)

couple of bob [1960s+] a reasonably large sum of money, usu. in phr. such as *that must have cost a couple ...*

curl-the-mo mazuma [1940s+] (Aus.) a great deal of money (*curl-the-mo*, curl the tips of one's moustache; Yid. *mazuma*, money)

English pluck [late 19C] money, esp. as used for gambling. thus phr. *have you any English pluck?*, have you the courage to gamble with me?

money's mammy [1930s+] (US underworld) a great deal of money

pocketful of rocks [mid-19C+] (US campus) money

At a Pecuniary Disadvantage

as full of money as a toad is of feathers [late 18C–19C]

beat for the yolk [1940s] (US Black/Harlem)

broke to the wide/world [1910s+]

cake is getting thin [20C] one's money is running low

can't hit a lick [1920s–30s] (US Black) used of an inability to succeed in a given aim, esp. that of making money either legally or otherwise

close to the blanket [1900s] (US)

devil may dance in his pocket [late 18C] said of one who has no money

down on/close to the knuckle(bone) [mid-19C–1930s]

gone with the wind [1930s+] vanished, esp. of money (pun on the 1939 film title)

having a bad case of the broke [1920s+] (US)

in hock [mid-19C+] indebted

What to Say when Caught in a Financially Embarrassing Circumstance

Sorry, mate, I ain't got a sixpence to scratch my arse with
[mid-19C+]

or one might, if of a more polite disposition, replace 'a sixpence to scratch my arse with' with

– a brass razoo [20C] (orig. N.Z., then Aus./N.Z.) *or*

– a feather to fly with [late 19C–1900s]

---

in the red [1920s+] in debt – although it can also mean 'in the money' (from the inking of old accounts, *red* for losses, black for profits)

let me hold some change [1960s+] (US Black) please give me some money

low in the lay [mid-19C–1910s]

on e. [1990s+] (US Black) (*on e*mpty)

on one's uppers [late 19C+]

on the back of one's arse [late 19C+] (Aus.)

on the hog (train) (also **on the pork**) [late 19C+] (US)

on the low gag [mid-19C]

on the outs [early 19C+]

on the picaro/picaroon [mid-19C] looking for a means of obtaining easy money (Sp. *picarón*, rogue)

on the ribs [1930s+]

on the rory [1970s+]

on the tap [20C] attempting to beg money

on the wallaby [mid-19C+]

out at elbows/heels [early 17C–late 19C]

pockets to let [19C]

shatting on one's uppers [late 19C+] (US)

short bread [1960s+] not enough cash

subscribing to the bookies' benefit [20C] betting recklessly and thus effectively donating one's money to the bookmakers

Poor as ...

– **a Connaught man** [late 19C] (Irish)

– **a drover's dog** [1940s+] (Aus.)

– **a rat** [early 18C+]

– **God's off-ox** [19C+] (US) (from SE *off-ox*, the ox harnessed to the *offside* of the team)

– **Job's turkey** [mid-19C+] (orig. US) (after the biblical *Job*, regarded as the personification of poverty)

– **Paddy Murphy's pig** [late 19C+] (US) (negative stereotyping of Irish immigrants)

The Secret Language of Business

c.r.e.a.m. [1990s+] (orig. US Black) money. i.e. 'cash
rules everything around me'

G.T.T. [late 19C] (US) gone to Texas; the sign affixed
to the door of an absconding businessman

o.p.m. [20C] (orig. US underworld) other people's
money, the ideal commodity in the eyes of any
entrepreneur; if one's deals fail, one loses nothing of
one's own; if they work out one is profiting without
investment; a staple of City or Wall Street jargon by
the 1980s

p.y.c. [20C] (Aus.) pay your cash.

s.r.o [20C] orig. entertainment use, a full house,
thus fig. anything that sells out or is very popular;
i.e. 'standing room only'

---

tapped out [1950s+] out of money, having nothing to use
for further betting

to the curb [1980s+] (synon. of SE phr. *in the gutter*)

tune the old cow died of [mid-19C+] a lecture or homily
delivered to a beggar instead of money

up a tree for tenpence [mid–late 19C]

without a mintie [1930s] (Aus.)

without a rag [late 16C+]

Not Short of a Bob or Two

beforehand with the world [mid-16C–18C] having money in reserve

do the lot [20C] to spend all one's available money

dripping with it [1920s+] abundant with, overloaded with, usu. in context of jewels or money

filthy with it [20C] full with, over-loaded with, usu. money

have a shot in one's locker [late 18C+] to have sufficient in reserve, e.g. money

meet sweet william [mid-19C–1900s] to pay off a bill as soon as it is presented

on the spend [late 19C+] spending money

that ain't hay [1930s+] that's a not insubstantial pile

MURDER *See* **VIOLENT AND UNTIMELY END, TO BRING ABOUT A**

N

NEGATION, ABSOLUTE

did I/do I/is it buggery!/fuck!/hell!/shit!/heck! [late 19C+]
e.g. *Did I steal that car? Did I fuck!* Similarly *Will I fuck!* = no,
I certainly won't

do I ducks! [20C] (euph. of *do I fuck!* see above)

fuck me drunk! [20C] (Aus.)

heck-of-a-no! [1990s+] (US teen)

like fucking hell! [late 19C+]

negatory! [1950s] (US, orig. milit.)

nix deberr! [early 19C] (Cockney) no, my friend (from
Ger. *nichts*, nothing + *deberr*, a perversion of Rus. *tovarich*,
a friend)

no fear! [mid-19C+] (orig. N.Z.)

no way! (also **no way José**, **no way in this world!**) [1960s+]
(orig. US)

no ta hey! [20C] (S.Afr.)

not bloody likely [late 19C+]

not by a dog's tail [20C] (US) not by a long way, in no way

not by a long shot [mid-19C+] (orig. US)

not in these boots [late 19C]

not in these trousers [1920s–30s]

not on your arse/ass! [1960s]

Not in these Trousers

not on your life! (also **not on your's**) [late 19C+]

not on your natural! [20C]

nothing doing (also **nothing stirrin'**) [early 19C+]

over my dead body [20C] in no possible way, never

In a Pig's Ass!

[20C] (orig. US) completely impossible! absolutely not!
I don't believe you! go away!

Also:

in a pig's ear!

in a pig's eye!

in a pig's hole!

in a pig's neck!

in a pig's pigs!

in a pig's poke!

in a pig's tonsil!

in a pig's valise!

in a pig's wig!

Not to mention:

in a bull's arse! [1950s]

in a cat's ass [1950s] (orig. US)

Snowballs in Hell: No Chance

fat chance [mid-19C+]

fat show! [1930s+] (N.Z.)

no hide, no Christmas box [1930s+] (Aus.)

When Pigs Fly...

no more chance than a cat in hell without claws [late 18C–mid-19C]

no more chance than a snowball/ice-cream cornet in hell [late 19C+]

no soap [1920s+] (orig. US)

not a fart's chance in a whirlwind [2000s]

No Good

Two bits of rhyming slang:
chump of wood [mid-19C]
no Robin Hood [1910s+] (orig. milit.)

not a ghost of a chance [mid-19C+]
not a hope in hell/the hot place [1910s+]
not a shit show [1980s+] (N.Z.)
not an earthly [mid-18C+]
not for all the tea/rice in China [late 19C+] (orig. Aus.)
not have a dog's/cat's chance [late 19C+]
not have a prayer [1940s+] (orig. US)
not on your nanny! [1950s+] (Anglo-Irish)
on a hiding to nothing [late 19C+] with absolutely no chance,
  esp. in a sporting contest
your name is Dennis [mid–late 19C] (US) you have no chance,
  you are finished, 'done for'
you will in your shite! [late 19C+] (Irish)

When Pigs Fly: Never
in a hog's horn [mid–late 19C] (US)
in the days/reign of Queen Dick [late 18C+]
not while pussy's a cat [20C] (Ulster)

on St Geoffrey's day [late 18C] (there is no St Geoffrey)

that'll be frosty Friday [1940s+] (Can./N.Z.)

when cock/fowl get/make teeth [20C] (W.I.)

when hens make holy water [17C]

when pigs fly [early 17C+]

when the devil is blind [mid-17C–1900s]

when the goose pisses/pisseth [early 18C–1900s]

when two Sundays meet/come together [mid–late 17C]

NERVOUS, ANXIOUS, AGITATED

See also DAZED AND CONFUSED; EMBARRASSING

all …

– hot and bothered [1920s+]

– in a twitter [late 18C+]

– of a jump [late 19C] (US)

– of a tremble [mid-18C–mid-19C]

– of a wonk [1910s+]

– revved up [1960s+]

fizzing at the bung/bunghole/slit [1990s]

flip one's cork/frijoles/noodle/raspberry/stack [1950s+]
(orig. US) to lose control, to get over-excited

in hot ashes [20C]

like a cat on a hot tin roof [20C]

like a cat on hot bricks [mid-19C+]

like a fart in a bottle/colander [late 19C+]

like a fly in a glue-pot/tar-box [mid-17C–late 19C]

like a hen/chicken on a hot griddle/plate [20C] (US)

off one's feed [mid-19C+]

on the …

– anxious bench/seat [19C] (US)

– carpet/mat [late 19C] (orig. US)

– edge [1970s+] (orig. US campus)

– go [late 17C]

– jump [mid-19C+]

– muscle (US) [mid-19C+]

shot full of holes [1910s+] (US) suffering a nervous breakdown

NONSENSE *See* STUFF AND NONSENSE

NO WORRIES

See also ADVISORY

all is bob [16C+] (UK underworld) everything's pleasant, satisfactory

… and Bob's your uncle [20C]

don't take on so [mid-19C+]

hang loose! [1950s+] (orig. US)

ish kabibble [1910s+] (US) it is of no importance to me, 'I should worry' (a Yiddish phr.)

it'll be all right on the night [late 19C+]

Like a Hen on a Hot Griddle

let me alone for that! [late 17C–late 19C] a general phr. of reassurance, 'you can trust me' or 'don't worry, everything will be fine'

no big deal [1960s+] (orig. US teen)

no flies (about) [mid–late 19C] (Aus.)

no stress [1990s+] (US campus)

no sweat [1950s+] (orig. US)

nothing to make a song and dance about [late 19C+]

O Pollaky! [late 19C] nonsense! rubbish! don't make such a fuss! (proper name of Ignatius 'Paddington' *Pollaky*, a celebrated contemporary private detective, with an office on Paddington Green, whose exploits, and surname, entered the common language; W.S. Gilbert also found room for him in a lyric, 'the keen penetration of Paddington Pollaky' (*Patience*, 1881). The phr. is also a euph. for the coarser excl. *oh bollocks!*)

she'll be right [1940s+] (Aus.)

stop trippin' over no luggage! [1990s] (US Black teen)

take it easy [mid-19C+]

that's cool [1950s+] (orig. US)

NUMERICAL PHRASES, A MOUNTING MISCELLANY OF

one-eyed boy with his shirtsleeves rolled up [1960s+] a circumcised penis

one for the bitumen [1940s] (Aus.) a last drink

one in the bush is worth two in the hand [1920s+] (Aus.)
one instance of proper intercourse is better than any amount
of masturbation

two looking at you [20C] (US) two fried eggs 'sunny side up'

two fat cheeks and ne'er a nose [18C] the backside

two-minute brother [1990s] (US Black) a man who suffers
from premature ejaculation

two stone under weight/wanting [late 18C–1900s] castrated;
thus a eunuch

two puppies fighting in a bag [1970s+] very large, poorly
contained and mobile breasts

three-letter man [1930s+] a homosexual; i.e. a *f-a-g*

three quarters of a peck [mid-19C] neck (rhy. sl.)

three tears and a bucket [1970s] (US Black) a expression of
dismissal or lack of interest

4-F Club [1950s+] a metaphorical 'club' based on the slogan
'*f*ind 'em, *f*eel 'em, *f*uck 'em and *f*orget 'em', the axiom for
macho US youth in its dealings with women

four sisters on thumb street [1970s+] (US Black) masturbation

fifth point of contact [1990s] (US) of a woman, the anus
(the other four points are the mouth, nipples and
vagina)

five against/on one [20C] masturbation

five and dime [20C] (US Black) paltry (from *five and dime*
stores)

five by five [1930s+] (US Black) a short, fat man (his girth
equals his height)

six blooming foot of tripe [late 19C] a large policeman

six months in front and nine behind [1930s–40s] (US Black) obese (from the resemblance of the fat person's stomach and buttocks to those of a pregnant woman)

six o'clock swill [1930s+] (Aus.) the rushed orders of drinks that, between 1916 and 1955 (before a change in the laws), took place in pubs in New South Wales before 'last orders'

six of everything [late 19C] respectable; used by working families to describe a woman about to be married (her trousseau has *six* sets *of everything* necessary)

six ways for Sunday [mid-19C] askew

seven kinds of hell [20C] intense unpleasantness; esp. in the phr. *knock/kick seven kinds of hell out of*, to beat severely

sevens and elevens [1910s+] (Can.) a satisfactory situation, esp. in the phr. *everything is/will be sevens and elevens*, everything is/will be fine (from use in the game of craps, 7 and 11 being the best points to achieve on one's initial throw)

seven-sided son of a bitch [19C] (US) a man or woman with one eye (he/she has a right side and a left side, a fore side and a backside, an outside, an inside and a blind side)

8-8-16 [20C] a prison cell (from the dimensions in inches of a single one of the blocks that make up the cell walls)

nine-inch knocker [20C] the penis

nine mile nuts [late 19C] anything sustaining, whether to eat or drink (from the supposedly nutritional properties of chestnuts)

ten miles of bad road [20C] (US Black) bad luck

tenpence to the shilling [mid-19C+] slightly eccentric or not very bright

ten pounds of shit in a five pound bag [20C] (US) anyone considered ugly, esp. someone who is obese

sixteen-year-old after shave [1970s] (US Black) very cheap and nasty wine

20 on the hype [1950s] (drugs) a very heavy intake of heroin.

twenty-three skid(d)oo [1890–1910] (US) go away! get out!; sometimes abbr. as *twenty-three!* (ety. unknown; one theory relates to the downdraughts created by the Flatiron Building at the corner of Broadway and 23rd Street, New York City, which would blow up women's skirts to the delight of male observers – the phr. developed from the police who saw these men at '23' (the corner) and shooed them away with a shout of *skiddoo*)

twenty-nine and a wake-up [1960s+] (US prison) the period between receiving a notice of parole and one's actual release, i.e. one month (29 whole days and the last, on which one only wakes up in jail)

38 hot [1990s] (US Black) extremely angry (from SE *38*, a .38 pistol + *hot*, angry)

forty miles of bad road [1960s+] an unattractive person, sight or situation

hundred to thirty [1970s] dirty (rhy. sl.)

OATHS AND GODLESS SWEARING

See also DISBELIEF, SURPRISE, ANNOYANCE, EXCLAMATIONS THEREOF; EUPHEMISMS

be/by the hokey! [late 18C+] (Irish) (var. on *by the holy poker!*)

be/by the holies! [20C] (Irish)

bless my soul! [19C]

blood and 'ounds! [late 19C–1900s] (i.e. *blood and wounds!*)

blow me tight [late 18C–1910s]

bullets and blisters! [mid–late 19C] (US)

burn my skin! [early–mid-19C] (US)

bust me! [mid–late 19C]

bust my gizzard! [mid-19C] (US)

cat's nouns! [early 18C] euph. for *God's wounds!*

cheese whiz! [1980s+] (US campus) a mild oath, synon.
of *gee whiz!*

Christ on a fire engine! [1990s]

cob's body! [early 18C] a euph. for *God's body!*

cor lumme! [mid-19C+] a euph. for *God love me!*

dammit to hell (and back)! [20C]

damn my sakes! [20C] (US)

damn my stars! [20C] (US)

dash my buttons! [mid-19C–1910s]

dash my wig! [late 18C–mid-19C]

dod rabbit it! [mid–late 19C] (US) euph. of 16C *God rebate it!*

dod rot it! [late 17C–late 19C] euph. of *God rot it!*

for God's sake! [mid-19C+]

for landsakes! [mid-19C+] (US) euph. of *for Lord's sake!*

gawd aggie! [20C] (Aus.)

go to Jerusalem! [19C]

Gosh

A euph. for God, *hence:*

gosh-almighty! [19C+]

gosh-damned! [19C+] (US)

gosh-darn! [19C+] (US) euph. for *God damn!*

gosh-ding! [mid-19C+] (US) as above

God has gone to Jersey City [1930s–40s] a mild oath, usu. in phr. *If I'm lying, then God has gone ...*

God's bodikins! [18C] lit. 'God's little body'

God's dines! [late 16C–early 17C]

God's trousers! [1900s–50s] (Aus.)

good gracious me! [18C+]

good strange! [early 18C] lit. 'God's strings'

goodness gracious! [19C+]

gracious alive/me! [19C+]

great Caesar ('s ghost)! [late 19C+] euph. for *great God!*

great scott! [19C+] ? as above or euph. for *great Satan*

great snakes! [19C+] (orig. US)

Od!

[late 16C+] a general euph., oath, meaning *God* and usu. found in a variety of combinations, e.g. *'od's blood, body, bones, death, feet, flesh, foot, life, mercy, truth, vengeance, blessed will, wounds* etc. Also with diminutions and perversions of words, as in *'od's bob, bobs, bodikins, bud* (= blood*), fish, 'odslid, odd's lifelings, odsnigs, ods-nouns, odsoons* (= wounds), *od's-pittikins, pittkins, pitlikins* (pity*), od's wucks, odzooks* (= hooks), *-zookers (-swookers), od zounds* (= wounds), *'od's haricots, kilderkins, od's my life*

I'll Be ...

- a Chinaman! [20C]
- a dirty word! [20C]
- a monkey's ass! [1970s] (US)
- consarned! [19C+]
- darned! [late 18C+] euph. for *I'll be damned!*
- jiggered! [early 19C+]

heavens to Betsy! [20C] (US)

hell with it! [20C]

in my stars! [17C]

jeepers creepers! [20C] euph. for *Jesus Christ!*

jeezle-peezle! [1970s+] (US) euph. for *Jesus!*

Jerusalem cricket(s)! (also Jerusalem June-bugs!) [mid-19C–1900s] (US) euph. for *Jesus Christ!*

Jesus H Christ! [late 19C+]

Jesus wept! [1920s+] (John 11:35, the shortest verse in the Bible)

kocks newnes! [mid-19C] euph. for *God's wounds!*

law sakes! [mid-19C+] (US) lit. 'for the Lord's sake!'

law's-a-me! [late 19C] (US) lit. 'Lord save me!'

lor-a-mussy! [19C] lit. 'Lord have mercy!'

lord love a duck! [20C]

lord love us! [late 19C+]

lord love your heart! [mid–late 19C]

may I gasp my last if ... [late 19C–1930s]

merciful hour! [1990s+] (Irish)

my cripes! [1910s+] euph. for *my Christ!*

my land! [mid-19C+] (Can./US)

my stars! [17C+]

nick me! [mid-18C]

odd rabbit! [mid-18C–late 19C] euph. for *God rot it!*

red peppers! [late 19C] (US)

s'elp my tater! [mid-19C–1900s]

shoot that hat! [mid-19C] (US)

split me! [late 17C–18C] an oath used by upper-class dandies

stap my vitals! [late 17C+] as above

suffering Christ! [late 19C+]

sweet (fucking) Jesus! [20C] (US)

Strike Me ...

- **blind!** [early 18C+]
- **blue!** [1910s+] (Aus./N.Z.)
- **dead!** [late 19C+]
- **lucky!** [mid-19C+] a general oath, esp. on the sealing of a bargain by slapping hands together

---

take my Bradlaugh [late 19C] take my oath, on my honour; thus *take one's Bradlaugh*, to swear an oath (the freethinker Charles *Bradlaugh* was tried for blasphemy in the 19C)

tare an' ages/ouns! [19C–1950s] (Irish) euph. for *tears and aches/wounds* (of Christ)

walking Moses! [1910s–20s]

ye gods (and little fishes)! [late 19C–1930s]

And after hearing all this one might say …

God forgive him the prayers he said [late 19C] phr. used when someone has been swearing long and loud

To which he or she might humbly respond:

pardon my French [1950s+] a 'genteel' euph., excuse my swearing

By …

– **all that's blue!** [mid-19C]

– **Cain!** [early–mid-19C] (US)

– **Christchurch!** [1940s+] (N.Z./UK) a euph. oath

– **cock and pie!** [mid-16C–mid-19C]

– **god's dines!** [late 16C–early 17C]

– **(good) gravy!** [mid-19C+] (US)

– **jacks/Jackson!** [late 19C+] euph. for *by Jesus!*

– **jiggers!** [late 19C] (orig. US) as above

– **jimminy!** [early 19C+] as above

– **by Joe!** [mid-19C–1940s] (US) as above

– **by Jove!** [late 16C+]

– **my cadaver!** [late 19C] (Cockney)

– **my hood!** [late 16C]

– **my 'sheath!** [mid-16C]

– **my truly!** [late 16C–late 18C] a mild oath, used to underpin the veracity of one's statement

– **our lakin!** [late 15C–mid-17C] euph. for *by our lady!*

– **the good Katty!** [19C] (UK/northern) a mild oath, *by the good (St) Catherine!*

– **the great horn spoon!** [mid-19C] (US)

– **the (great) jumping Judas!** [20C] (US)

– **the holy jumping mother of Moses** [late 19C]

– **the holy poker (and the tumbling Tom)!** [19C]

– **the Lord Harry!** [17C–19C] (ref. to Old *Harry*, the devil)

– **the mack!** [mid-16C–mid-17C] ? euph. for *mass* or *Mary*

– **the piper that played before Moses** [late 19C]

– **the powers of Moll Doyle!** [mid-19C+] (Irish) (from *Moll Doyle's Daughters*, a clandestine agrarian society, pitted against rapacious landlords and similar figures)

– **these ten bones** [late 15C–early 16C] i.e. by the fingers of both hands

Holy ...

– **balls!** [1940s+] (orig. US)

– **bilge water!** [20C]

– **cow!** [1920s+] (orig. US)

– **crap!** [1960s+] (US)

– **cripes!** [20C]

– **crow!** [1960s+] (US)

- **dooley!** [20C] (Aus.)
- **fly!** [20C] (Irish)
- **fuck!** [1940s+] (orig. US)
- **kicker!** [late 19C+]
- **moly!** [1940s+] a variant on *Holy Moses*, favoured as a catchphrase by the comic-book hero Captain Marvel
- **poker!** [20C] (Irish)
- **shit!** [1950s+]
- **show!** [mid-19C–1900s]
- **smoke!** [late 19C+]
- **snapping duck shit!** [20C] (Aus.)

P

POVERTY *See* **MONEY**

PREGNANT

away the trip [20C] (Scot.)

full of it [late 19C]

have a bellyful of marrow-pudding [mid-19C]

how-come-ye-so [19C–1910s]

in a delicate condition/state of health [mid-19C]

in a fix [20C] (US)

in the club [20C]

in the familiar way [late 19C]

in the family way [18C+]

in the flue (also up the flue) [1930s]

in the pudding club [1930s+]

in the spud line [1930s+]

like that [1970s+] (US, mainly South)

martin's hammer knocking at the wicket [18C–19C]
pregnant with twins (Father *Martin*, a man with a staff;
the link to twins is unknown)

Mr Knap is concerned (also **Mr Knap has been there**)
[early 19C] (from sl. *knap*, to steal)

on the hill [1950s+] (US)

on the nest [20C] (US)

on the stick [1940s+] (orig. Aus.)

on the way [late 16C+]

pudding in the oven [1940s+]

pu the elop [20C] (backsl., 'up the pole')

run to seed [mid-19C]

shot in the tail [20C]

spitting at the tongs [20C] (Ulster)

the rabbit died [1950s+]

thickening for something [1950s+]

up ...

– **the creek (without a paddle)** [1930s+] (Aus.)

– **the duff** [1940s+] (orig. Aus.)

– **the kite** [1990s+]

– **the pole** [1920s+]

– **the spout** [early 19C–1920s]

– **the way** [20C] (Aus.)

To Become Pregnant

break one's ankle [late 18C+]

burn one's foot [20C] (US)

eat dried apples [20C] (US) i.e. to swell up like dried fruit placed in water

eat pumpkin seeds [20C] (US)

get into trouble [early 19C+]

hit on the master-vein [17C]

make feet for children's shoes [1930s+] (US Black)

sprain one's ankle [late 18C+] to become pregnant out of wedlock

swallow a watermelon seed [20C] (US)

PRISON

See also CRIME AND THE UNDERWORLD

Doing Time

do [mid-19C+] to serve a sentence in prison, usu. in phr. *do life, do five years*

A variety of expressions denote different sentences and punishments:

acre (of corn) [1940s+] (Aus.) a lengthy prison sentence, cited variously as one month, 12 months or simply 'plenty'; thus the phr. used of a recidivist, **there's corn growing for some**

all day from a quarter [20C] (US underworld) a sentence of 25 years to life

bullet [1960s+] (US prison) a one-year sentence

cake and wine [1920s] (US prison) bread and water

clock [1950s–60s] (Aus.) a one-year sentence

in the peek [1940s–50s] (UK prison) in an observation cell, into which prisoners are placed if, for instance, they have smashed up their cells or shown other signs of instability

night on the city [1970s] (US) a night in prison

on the shelf [19C+] (US prison) in solitary confinement

ride old smokey [1920s–60s] (US prison) to be electrocuted

stunned on skilly [mid-19C] (UK underworld) sent to prison and thus forced to endure a diet of gruel

take a walk up back [1920s] (US prison) to be moved from one's cell to the execution chamber

Going to and Staying in Prison

brought/go to the basket [early 17C–early 18C]

down the chute [1920s+] (Aus.)

down the river [late 19C+]

go up the river [late 19C+]

in the cold [1910s+] (Aus.)

in the hospital [1900s–20s] (US)

in the mix [1990s+] (US prison)

lying in state [1920s] (US prison)

on ice [1930s+]

out of town [early 19C]

out to pasture [20C] (US underworld)

under the hatches [late 17C–19C]

under the screw [mid-19C]

under wraps [1930s+]

up the river [20C] (orig. US)

Leaving Prison (Lawfully)

back-gate parole [1920s+] an inmate's death in prison

flop [1910s–50s] (US) a sleep, esp. a prisoner's last night in prison

hit the road [late 19C+] leave prison

on the bricks/ground [20C] (US) on the street after being released from prison

on the outs (also **on the out**) [early 19C+] (UK/US underworld) out of prison

on the street [mid-19C+] (orig. US) out of prison, in public life

Leaving Prison (Unlawfully)

To escape:

blow [late 19C] (US prison)

do a cross-country [1920s] (US prison)

fly the coop [mid-19C+]

mill a quod [mid-18C–late 19C]

To be on the run:

absent without leave [mid-19C+]

on the hop [20C] (US prison)

on the hot [1930s–40s] (US underworld)

on the jump [mid-19C+] (US underworld)

on the lam [1920s+] (US underworld)

over the wall [1930s+]

QUIET, PLEASE

belt up! [1930s+] (orig. RAF)

bite the bag! [1950s+] (US campus)

chain up! [1920s] (fig. use of phr. *chain up* that dog)

cheese it! [early 19C+]

close your head! [1930s–40s]

dry up! [mid-19C+]

edge it! [20C] (Aus.)

gerry gan! [16C] lit. 'shit in your mouth'

get back into your box! [late 19C+] (orig. US)

give us a rest! [late 19C+] (US)

hold it down! [20C]

hold the blow! [18C+]

if I want any shit from you, I'll squeeze your head [20C] (Aus.)

keep your trap shut [late 18C+]

knock it off! [late 19C+]

lay down! [1920s–30s] (US)

less it! [1970s+] (UK juv.)

let the priest say mass [20C] (Irish)

mash that! [late 19C] (from ? Fr. *macher*, to chew (on))

mum your dubber! [late 18C]

nantee palaver! [mid-19C+] (from Ital. *niente*, nothing + Port. *palabra*, speech, talk)

peter that! [19C]

pipe down! [late 19C+]

put a cork in it! [1980s+] (US)

*Close
Your
Head*

Shut Your ....

– **beak!** [20C] (W.I.)
– **can!** [1910s] (US)
– **gobble!** [late 19C]
– **head/neck** [19C] (US)
– **rag-box!** [late 19C]
– **shop!** [mid–late 19C]
– **mouth and give your ass a rest** [20C]

Hold Your ...

– **hush** [18C+]
– **jaw** [18C+]
– **mouth** [18C+]
– **mud** [1960s+] (US)
– **whid** [mid-19C] (*whid* = word)
– **whiz** [late 19C–1920s]

put it up! [mid-19C]
put your head in a bag! [late 19C+]
ring off! [late 19C–1920s]
save it! [1950s+] (US)

shoot that! [late 19C–1900s]

shut it! [late 19C+]

shut up! [mid-19C+]

slacken your glib! [late 19C]

stop your gab! [early 19C–1900s]

stop your gap! [late 19C+]

stow it/your noise/your yap! [mid-16C–mid-19C]

stow magging! [19C]

stubble it! [late 17C–19C] (UK underworld)

switch off! [1900s–20s]

tace is Latin for a candle [late 17C–early 19C] (from Lat.
tace, be silent + the snuffing out of a candle)

take a red-hot potato! [mid-19C]

turf it! [1930s+] (Aus.)

who are you? [1980s+]

zip it up! [1930s+]

S

SARTORIAL MATTERS

Looking Good

all dolled up like a barber's cat [mid–late 19C] (Can.)

as cool as a moose [1960s+]

bang up to the mark (also **bang up to dick**) [early 19C+]
first-rate, excellent, fashionable, stylish

busting out [1990s] (US Black)

clean and ready [20C] (US Black)

clean to the bone (also **ragged to the bone**) [1930s+] (US Black)

cool as a moose [1960s+]

diked up (also **dyked up, diked out**) [mid-19C+] (US)

dogged out/up [1910s+] (orig. US)

dressed to kill [early 19C+]

All Dolled Up Like a Barber's Cat

dressed (up) like a deacon [20C] (US)

dressed up to the knocker [19C]

dressed (up) to the nines [mid-19C+]

fonky to the bone [1940s+] (US Black)

groomed to zoom [1970s] (US campus)

hip to the tip [20C] (US Black)

in full fig [19C+]

in full paint [1900s] (Aus.)

in one's gears [late 17C–early 18C]

laid/mod to the bone [1960s–70s] (US Black)

The Secret Language of Clothes

m.d.l. [1990s] a woman who dresses younger than her years; i.e. '*m*utton *d*ressed as *l*amb'

p.i.b. [1990s] (US campus) a brooding, gloomy adolescent who wears dark clothes and listens to gloomy alternative music; i.e. '*p*eople *i*n *b*lack'

p.d.k. [1980s+] (US campus) someone who is out of fashion; i.e. '*p*olyester *d*ouble-*k*nit'

v.b.c. [1980s+] (US campus) having the outline of one's buttocks showing through tight trousers; or revealing the top of one's buttocks due to wearing one's trousers lower than the waist; i.e. '*v*isible *b*utt *c*rack'

v.p.l. [1980s+] *v*isible *p*anty *l*ine

---

sharp as a mosquito's peter [1970s+] (US Black)

sharp as a rat turd [20C]

smart as a carrot new scraped [late 18C–mid-19C]

totally Penelope Pitstop [1990s] (US teen)

up to the knocker [mid–late 19C]

Trying Too Hard

However, if you overdo it, you might be described as …

all laired up [1920s+] (Aus.) flashily dressed

all mockered up [1940s+] (Aus.) as above

or as a …

Christmas tree [20C] (US) a heavily over-made-up or over-dressed woman

… while others might say you are **dressed up like a …**

– **dog's dinner** [1930s+]

– **pox doctor's clerk** [1950s+] (Aus.)

– **sore finger** [20C] (Aus./N.Z./US)

Indeed, urchins in the street might shout …

going to keep a piano shop? [late 19C] a mocking phr. directed at anyone the speaker feels is over-well-dressed, even flashy

And if your hair is too long as well, they might add …

where's your violin? [1940s+] (Aus.)

who robbed the barber? [late 19C–1910s]

Smart as ...

– **a rat with a gold tooth** [20C] (Aus.)
– **be-damned** [1920s–30s]
– **threepence** [late 19C]

Got up ...

– **regardless**
– **to kill**
– **to the knocker**
– **to the nines**

SEX, MOSTLY

See also EUPHEMISMS: MASTURBATION; MATRIMONY

Flirting and Courting

act the linnet [20C] (Irish)
breast up to [1910s+] (Aus.)
buck up to [19C] (US)
carry on [mid-19C] (orig. US)
cart out with [late 19C+]
catch under the pinny [1900s–30s]

Like a
Dog's Dinner

come on to [1960s+] (orig. US)

cop on [late 19C+] (Ulster)

cop one's drawers [1960s+] (US)

drop one's wing [19C] (US Black) (a bird lures another by dropping a wing)

feature with [1960s+] (orig. Aus.)

fire into [20C]

fly a kite at [mid-19C]

give someone some play [1970s+] (US Black)

give the heat [1930s+]

go in for [mid–late 19C] (orig. US)

grab on [1980s+] (US campus)

hang one's hat up to [mid-19C–1900s] i.e. while visiting the beloved

hit on [1940s+] (US)

hoopdie swoop [1970s+] (US Black)

horse around [1950s+] (US)

knob on to [late 19C–1920s]

knock over [1940s–60s] (US)

line up [1940s+] (Aus.) lit. 'to accost'

make a hole in someone's reputation [mid-19C+]

make a play for [20C]

make mack with [1960s+] (US Black) lit. to act like a pimp

make time with [1930s+] (US)

pull the cord [late 19C] (Anglo-Irish)

put a move/the moves on [1960s+] (orig. US)

put someone away [1950s+] (orig. US)
put the hard word on [20C] (Aus.)
put the make on [1950s+] (US)
reel in the biscuit [1970s+] (US campus)
run a game on/run game on [1940s+] (US Black)
run down [20C] (W.I.)
schmiel on [1980s+] (US campus)
scoop on [1980s+] (US campus)
stick up to [1900s] (N.Z.)
strike out [20C] (US)
sweet talk [1930s+] (orig. US Black)
talk shit [1930s+] (US Black)
tell the tale [20C]
tiddle a girl [mid-19C+] lit. 'to fondle'
wire in and get one's name up [mid–late 19C]

Awkward Social Situations No. 10

What to Say to an Over-Attentive Wooer

you shakin' yo' drawers in ma face? [1930s] (US Black)
*or one might, wary of missing an opportunity, more directly
  inquire:*
wanna root? [20C] (Aus.)

The Secret Language of Dating

d.d.f.m.g. [1990s] (US campus) excl. on sighting a very attractive member of the opposite sex; i.e. 'drop dead fuck-me gorgeous'

D.L.C. [1980s+] (US campus) deep, heavy conversation; down low conversation

D. & M. [1990s] (US teen) a deep and meaningful conversation

m.d.g. [1980s+] (US campus) strong physical attraction; i.e. 'mutual desire to grope'

m.l.a. [1990s] (US campus) passionate kissing; i.e. 'massive lip action'

m.o.s. [1980s+] (US campus) member of the opposite sex

m.o.y. [1980s+] my place or yours?

n.g.b. [1980s+] (US campus) a pleasant person, but not one with whom one wishes to have a sexual relationship; i.e. 'nice guy but'

n.t.o. [1990s] (US campus) a date who does not come up to expectations; i.e. 'not the one'

n.t.s. [1970s+] (US campus) attractive male that makes a female's heart beat so fast that her name tag shakes; i.e. 'name tag shaker'

o.a.o. [1920s+] (orig. US) one's steady girlfriend; i.e. 'one and only'

p.d.a. [1980s] (US 'preppie') kissing and cuddling in public; public display of affection

p.p.d. [1980s+] (US campus) an attractive person of the opposite sex; i.e. 'possible/potential prom date'

v.b.d. [1960s] (US Black) an unsatisfactory evening with a member of the opposite sex; i.e. 'very bad date'

Getting Somewhere

getting ...

– **a bit** [20C]

– **across** [1920s–60s] (US Black)

– **among it** [1910s+] (Aus.)

– **among the frills** [late 19C–1910s]

– **a time with** [20C] (W.I.)

– **into** [early 19C+]

– **into someone's pants** [1960s+]

– **it on** [1950s+] (orig. US Black)

– **next to** [1940s+] (US Black)

– **off with** [1910s+]

– **one's leg across/over** [early 18C+]

– **over** [late 19C–1910s]

Foreplay and Fiveplay

feel one's way to heaven [19C]

finger-fuck [mid-19C+]

get a handful of sprats [late 19C+] (alluding to the 'fishiness' of the vagina)

make out [1940s+] (US)

peck and neck [1970s] (US Black)

play stinkfinger [late 19C+]

tip the little/middle/long finger [19C]

tip the long 'un [late 19C–1900s]

warm up [1970s+]

Having Sex

ball slapping [1990s]

beating with an ugly stick [1980s+] (US campus)

bouncing refrigerators [1980s+] (US campus)

bumping ...

– **bellies** [20C] (US)

– **fuzz** [1980s+] (US campus)

– **uglies** [1970s+] (US Black/teen)

bussin cunu [20C] (W.I.) lit. 'breaking cunt'

busting/beating one's nuts [1940s+]

busting some booty/someone out [1980s+] (US Black)

carving a slice [20C]

cutting the mustard [20C]

dipping the schnitzel [20C]

doing a kindness [20C]

doing the humpty-bump [1990s] (US campus)

doing the naked pretzel [1990s+] (US campus)

doing the nasty [20C]

doing the natural thing [20C]

drilling for oil [1940s] (orig. US Black)

getting one's hole [1960s+]

getting up to ya nuts in guts [20C] (Aus.)

going ...

– **nesting** [20C]

– **bottom hole working** [20C]

- **pop like a paper bag** [1950s+] copulating with great
  enthusiasm
grinding one's coffee [1920s] (US)
hauling one's ashes [20C]
hitting skins [20C]
laying some pipe [1930s+] (US)
making her grunt [20C]
making her scream [1980s+] (US campus)
parking the pink cadillac [1990s]
peeling one's best end in [late 19C–1910s]
playing fathers and mothers [20C]
playing hide the salami [20C]
playing night baseball [20C]
ploughing the back forty [1950s+] (US)
polishing one's arse on the top sheet [20C]
popping it in [late 19C+]

Donald Ducking

Some rhyming slang euphs. for 'fuck':
Donald Duck [1960s+] (Aus.)
friar tuck [late 19C+]
goose and duck [late 19C+]
trolley and truck [1910s+]

---

potting the white [1930s+]

putting barney in the VCR (US Black) (*VCR*, video cassette recorder)

putting it in and breaking it [20C]

ripping off a piece [1950s+] (US)

rocking one's world [1980s+] (US campus)

sawing off a chunk/length/piece [1960s+]

Getting ...

- **a shot of crack/leg** [20C] (US)
- **gravel for one's goose** [1930s+] (US)
- **on the old fork** [late 19C–1900s]
- **one's agates cracked** [1940s+] (US)
- **one's axle greased** [1960s]
- **one's banana peeled** [late 19C+] (orig. US)
- **one's batteries charged** [1930s+] (US)
- **one's corn ground** [early 19C] (US)
- **one's dipper wet** [1980s+] (US)
- **one's lance waxed** [1980s]
- **one's rocks off** [1940s+]
- **one's swerve on** [1970s] (US Black)
- **shot in the tail** [late 17C–early 18C]
- **some pink** [1990s] (US)

Spearing the Bearded Clam

scoring between the posts [20C]

shaking a tart [late 19C+]

sinking the little man in the boat/the soldier [20C]

skinning the cat [19C+]

skinning the pizzle [mid-19C–1900s] (from *pizzle*, orig. bull's penis)

slapping skins [1990s] (orig. US Black)

socking it to someone [1960s] (orig. US Black)

spearing the bearded clam [1960s+] (Aus.)

Slipping and Sliding

slipping ...
– her a length [1940s+]
– her a quick crippler [1940s+]
– in Daintie Davie [19C] (Scot.)
– in Willie Wallace [19C] (Scot.)
– it to her [1940s+]

---

spearing the hairy doughnut [1990s]
splitting the difference [1970s]
squeezing one's/the lemon [1930s+] (orig. US Black)
stabbing in the main vein [1950s+]
tearing off a bit/chunk [1970s+]
tearing off a piece [1940s+] (orig. Aus.)
varnishing the cane [late 19C–1960s] (US)
waxing some ass [1970s+] (US Black)
winding one's ball of yarn [20C]
working one's bot [20C]
During all this, one might merrily enjoin:
whip that thing! [1940s+] (US Black) a cry of pleasure
  and encouragement during sexual intercourse
And after it all one might declare that one is ...
a.f.o. [20C] i.e. '*all fucked out*'

Animal Images and Bestial Pleasures

doing a bit of ...

– cock-fighting [19C]

exercising the ferret [1960s+]

going cunny-catching [18C] (from *cunny*, rabbit, with pun on *cunt*)

greasing the weasel [1990s] (US teen)

having a bit of ...

– fish on a fork [mid-19C–1900s]

– rabbit-pie [19C]

leading the llama to the lift shaft [1990s]

playing at cock in cover [19C]

playing stable my naggie [18C–19C]

playing the goat [18C]

putting on dog [mid-19C+] (US)

riding the hobby horse [1980s+] (US campus)

slinging fish [1980s+] (US)

sticking one's duck in the mud [1970s] (US)

tethering one's nags (on someone) [19C] (Scot.)

(More) Dirty Dancing

To have sex is to dance ...

– on the mattress [19C]

– the blanket hornpipe [19C]

– the buttock jig [19C]

– the goat's jig [19C]

– **among her frills** [19C]

– **among the cabbages** [19C]

– **among the parsley** [19C]

– **in Bushey Park** [19C]

– **in Cock Alley** [19C]

– **in Cock Lane** [19C]

– **in Cupid's Alley** [19C]

– **in Cupid's Corner** [19C]

– **in Hair Court** [19C]

– **in Love Lane** [19C]

– **on Mount Pleasant** [19C]

– **on Shooter's Hill** [1970s] (US Black)

– **through the stubble** [18C–19C]

– **up her petticoats** [19C]

– **the married man's cotillion** [19C]

– **the matrimonial polka** [19C]

– **the mattress jig** [19C]

– **the miller's reel** [19C]

– **to the tune of shaking the sheets (without music)** [19C]

– **with your arse to the ceiling** [19C]

Sexual intercourse can be **horizontal** ...
– **barn-dancing** [1950s+]
– **mambo** [1950s+]
– **polka** [1950s+]
– **rhumba** [1950s+]

National Styles

American culture [1960s+] 'straight' intercourse
Chinese fashion [1960s+] on one's side
English culture [1960s+] bondage and discipline
Greek culture [1930s+] anal sex
Roman culture [1960s+] orgies
Swedish culture [1960s+] rubber fetishism

We Hae Meat and We Can Eat, So Let the Lord be Thankit

bury the brisket [1950s+] (US)
cut a side [late 18C+]
cut a slice off the joint [late 18C+]
give someone some meat [1950s+]
have/do a bit of beef [late 19C+]
have a bit of giblet pie [19C]
have a bit of meat [late 19C+]
have a bit of mutton [mid-16C+]
have a bit of pork [18C+]
have a bit of split mutton [18C–1900s]

have a bit off the chump end [20C]

have a jumble-giblets [17C]

hide one's/the baloney [1920s+]

hide the sausage [1940s+]

hide the weenie/wienie [1920s+]

join giblets [18C]

mash the fat [1970s+] (US Black)

pour the pork [1950s+] (orig. US)

pull the bacon [1990s]

put four quarters on the spit [18C] i.e. the participants' limbs

put the meat to [20C]

rub offal [1990s+]

sink the sausage [1980s+]

stir the stew [1900s–10s]

stretch some meat [1980s+] (US)

From the Female Angle

catch an oyster [19C]

do a back fall [19C]

do a spread [mid-19C]

do a tumble [1900s]

do a wet bottom [19C]

do the naughty [1950s+] (Aus./N.Z.)

do what mother did before me [19C]

drop one's tweeds [20C]

feed one's pussy [20C]

get a bellyful of marrow pudding [mid-19C]

get a bit of goose's neck [late 19C]

get a go at the creamstick [19C+]

get a handle for the broom [19C]

get a shove in one's blind eye [late 18C–1900s]

get one's chimney swept (out) [19C]

get one's kettle mended [17C]

get one's leather stretched [18C+]

get one's leg lifted [early 18C–late 19C]

get outside/outside of [late 19C+]

get shot in the tail [late 17C–early 18C]

give juice for jelly [19C]

give mutton for beef [19C]

give soft for hard [19C]

give standing room for one only [19C]

have a bit of sugar stick [19C]

have a live sausage for supper [19C]

look at the ceiling [20C]

lose the match and pocket the stakes [19C]

pray with one's knees upwards [late 18C–early 19C]

ride a St George [19C] (when the woman is on top)

ride the baloney pony [1990s] (US)

take in and do for [mid-19C]

turn up one's tail [late 17C–early 18C]

Riding the Baloney Pony

Making the Beast with Two Backs: A Chronolog-icalle Miscellanie of Ye Olde Rumpie-Pumpie

16th Century:

fleshing it

groping for trout in a peculiar river

making the beast with two backs

shaking a skin-coat

17th century:

blowing off the loose corns

blowing the groundsels

going ...

– fleshmongering

– on Hobbes' voyage (the writer's last words were of 'a great
 leap in the dark')

– prickscouring

– tail-tickling

– tail-twitching

jumping up and down

lapping clap

making a settlement in tail (play on legal term 'entail')

playing at pickle-me-tickle-me

18th Century:

Adam and Eve-ing it

dropping one's load

emptying one's trash

engaging in/playing at three to one (and bound to lose)

going …
– beard-splitting
– bum-fighting/faking/tickling/working
– buttock-stirring
– face-making (i.e. the *face* of a new baby)
joining paunches
labouring/stretching leather
nailing two wames together (Scot. *wame*, the belly)
shaking the sheets
winding up the clock
working the hairy oracle

19th Century:
dipping one's wick
dipping the fly
diving into the dark
doing a bit of front-door work
feeding the dumb glutton/dummy
getting jack in the orchard
getting one's greens
going…
– quim-sticking/wedging
– rump splitting
– to Hairyfordshire
– under petticoating
having a bit of bum
jumping someone's/on someone's bones

playing a tune on the one-holed flute

playing at mumble-peg (lit. 'a game in which each player in turn throws a knife, continuing until they fail to make the blade stick in the ground')

putting the devil into hell

riding below the crupper

seeing the stars lying on one's back (of a woman)

stabbing in the thigh

stropping one's beak

taking Nebuchadnezzar out to grass (the Babylonian king who 'liked his greens')

walloping it in

whacking it up

To Deflower

crack a Judy/Judy's tea-cup [early 19C+]

cut the cake [20C] (US Black)

have a cherry [1920s+] (US)

pierce the hogshead [17C]

pluck a rose [17C+]

pop a/someone's cherry [1950s+] (orig. US)

scuttle a ship [19C]

split the cup [1970s] (US Black)

tap a girl [late 18C–early 19C]

tap a judy [mid–late 19C]

trim the buff [late 18C]

To Reach Orgasm

blast off [1960s](US)

blow/pop one's ...

– cork [1930s+] (US)

– hump [1950s+] (US)

– juice [1990s]

– load [1990s]

– lot [1940s+] (Aus.)

– tubes [1990s]

bust one's kicks off [1920s+] (US)

bust/beat one's nut/nuts [1940s+] (US)

crack one's marbles [1930s] (US)

crack one's nuts [1940s–60s] (US)

fire a shot [late 19C+]

get home [19C]

get ...

– off [1970s+] (orig. US Black)

– off the button [1930s] (US)

– one's balls off [1960s+] (orig. US)

– one's cookies [1950s+]

– one's gun/gun off [1960s+]

– one's jones off [1960s+] (orig. US Black)

– one's kicks off [1920s+] (US)

– one's nuts off [1930s+] (orig. US Black)

– one's rocks off [1940s+]

go up the rainbow [1970s]

light up [1940s–50s]

make one's love come down [1950s–60s] (US Black)

make the chimney smoke [mid-19C+]

ready to spit [20C]

shoot one's rocks [1940s+]

To Give Someone an Orgasm

bring on the china [1900s–30s]

bring someone off [20C]

bust someone out [1980s+] (US Black)

do her job for her [mid-19C+]

give one's gravy [19C]

give someone a thrill [1910s+]

pop someone off [1950s+] (orig. US)

pop someone's cookies [1970s+]

pop someone's nuts [1950s+]

ring someone's bell [1910s+]

ring someone's chimes [1970s+] (orig. US)

Not Having Sex

aching for a side of beef [1970s+] (US Black) of a woman,
  eager to have sex

after one's greens [late 19C] of a man, sexually eager

as toey as a roman sandal [1930s+] (Aus.) in need of sex

b.a.v. [1980s+] (US campus) one who has not had sexual
  intercourse for a long time; i.e. 'born again virgin'

in a bad way [1960s] (US campus) sexually frustrated

on the carpet [late 19C+] (US) of someone who is eager to marry, esp. a widow or widower

on the make (orig. US) [mid-19C+] seeking sexual activity

Man-to-Man Talk

betty rub! [1980s+] (US campus) used by one male to another, meaning 'you're going to get lucky with her'

does she? [late 19C+] a comment passed by men on an adjacent woman, the implication being, *does she* fuck?

don't fancy yours! [20C] a joking reflex comment when two young men see two women, irrespective of their real charms

fuck one's/the arse/ass off/brains out [1950s+] to copulate enthusiastically, from the male point of view; often in wishful phr. voiced by a young man watching a passing woman, 'I could/I'd like to fuck the arse off that'

getting any (lately)? [1940s+] (orig. Aus.) a popular greeting between men

if they're old enough to bleed, they're old enough to butcher (also **if they're big enough to bleed, they're big enough to butcher**) [1960s+] a phr. used among men to suggest that if a girl is old enough to menstruate she is old enough for intercourse

I wouldn't kick her out of bed [20C] ref. to an attractive woman; a comment usu. made by one of a group of young men observing a passing woman

twelve o'clock high, check it out [1980s+] (US campus) used to focus attention on someone in a group for the purpose of sex or romance

up her like a rat up a drain(pipe) [1960s+] (orig. Aus.) the
assumption that a woman will be freely, easily and speedily
sexually available to the speaker

you don't look at the mantelpiece when you're poking the fire
[20C] meaning a woman's looks are irrelevant if she is
sexually available

Promiscuous Persons

always in trouble like a Drury Lane whore [late 19C+]

bangs like a dunny door in a storm [1950s+] (Aus.)

cheesy, sleazy, greasy [1980s+] (US campus)

common as a barber's chair [18C]

he'd fuck anything with a hole in it [20C]

he gets more ass than a toilet seat [1940s+] (orig. US)

he gets more butt than ashtrays [1940s+] (US)

lawless as a town bull [late 17C–early 19C] said of a
promiscuous man

Little Miss Roundheels [1950s+]

loose in the/her rump [18C–mid-19C]

no better than he/she should be [late 19C+]

she'll go for/fuck/have anything in trousers [late 19C+]

she's had more meat through her than an abattoir [1940s+]
(Aus.)

she's had more pricks than a second-hand dartboard [1940s+]
(Aus.)

Unsatisfactory Partners of Either Sex

bad shag [late 18C–early 19C] an unsatisfactory lover, usu. in the phr. **he is but bad shag**

free of fumbler's hall [late 17C–18C] referring to an impotent husband

love 'em and leave 'em [late 19C+] philandering, womanizing, e.g. 'he's the love 'em and leave 'em sort'

off the runway [1990s+] (US campus) used of a very thin girl (the imagery of the catwalk or *runway* down which ultra-thin supermodels parade)

Satisfactory Partners of Either Sex

Attractive and/or capable women:

bangs like a hammer on a nail [1950s+] (orig. Aus.) rates as an enthusiastic sexual performer

fuck like a mink [1910s+] (Aus./US) of a woman, to copulate enthusiastically

go like a rabbit [1950s+] as above

go like a train [20C] as above

go off like a two-bob watch [1960s+] (Aus.) of a woman, to be highly sexed

whacko the diddle-oh! [1960s+] (Aus.) a general excl. of pleasure, esp. on seeing an attractive woman

Attractive and/or capable men:

fuck like a rattlesnake [20C] of a man, to copulate enthusiastically

go in and out like a fiddler's elbow [20C] to copulate enthusiastically and energetically

he could make me write bad checks [1980s+] (US campus) a comment made by a woman about an especially attractive man

hot and heavy like a tailor's goose [late 17C–18C] applied to a passionate lover

Endowments Great and Small

built like a tripod [1990s] (US) having a large penis

have balls on one like a scoutmaster [1930s+] (Can./N.Z.) to have large testicles

hung like a horse/(jack) donkey/mule/stallion/show dog/hoover hose/stud [1960s+] possessing a large penis

hung like a (field) mouse/hamster/humming bird/a (stud) mosquito [1960s+] possessing an extremely small penis

The Secret Language of Sex

a.w.o.l. [1980s] *a*mour *w*ithout *lo*ve, used by habituées of singles bars to denote their brief (strictly sexual) entanglements

b.o.a.t. [1980s] a semi-professional prostitute, whose clients tend to be wealthy and whose payments are often less obvious than mere cash; i.e. '*b*ordering *o*n *a t*art'

B.S.Hs. [1960s–70s] the female breasts; i.e. '*B*ritish *S*tandard *H*andfuls', a pun on the *BSI*, British Standards Institution

c.b. [1970s+] *c*ock and *b*alls; used in S&M contact ads to advertise 'cock and balls torture'

c.c.c. [1990s] red female pubic hair; i.e. '*c*opper *c*oloured *c*unt/*c*rack'

c.f.m. [1980s+] (US) sexually suggestive; i.e. '*c*ome *f*uck *me*', thus *c.f.m. shoes, c.f.m. frock* etc.

A Well-Endowed Scoutmaster

c.o.d. [1960s+] a male whore; i.e. *cock on delivery*, punning on *C.O.D.*, *cash on delivery*

c.p.s.i. [1990s] *cunt per square inch*; usu.in the phrase *more c.p.s.i. in ... than ...* , and defining a place where there is a good chance of picking up girls

c.s.p. [1980s+] (US campus) a *casual sex partner*

c.y.t. [1920s+] an attractive young girl; i.e. '*cute young thing*'

D.O.M. [1950s+] *Dirty Old Man*

f.s. [1960s] a woman who offers oral sex; i.e. '*face-sitter*'

g.i.b. [1940s+] (orig. Aus./US) of a woman, *good in bed*

O.M.O. [1960s+] a signal used by a part-time or amateur prostitute, denoted by the placing of a packet of the washing-powder Omo in the window, indicating that the husband is away at sea and the woman is therefore available for sex; i.e. '*Old Man Out*'

o.n.e. [1980s+] *one night's experience*

p.e.e.p. [20C] the vagina; i.e. '*perfectly elegant eating pussy*'

p.h.a. [1990s] the penis; i.e. '*purple-headed avenger*'

p.p. [1920s+] of a man, having an erection on awakening; i.e. '*piss-proud*'

s.f.&t. [1990s] *sucked, fucked, and tattooed*

s.m.s. [1990s] (US campus) fellatio; i.e. '*suckle my sac*'

s.o.t.'s [1990s] a Wonderbra, designed to enhance one's cleavage; i.e. '*strap-on tits*'

s.t.o.l. [1980s] a brief sexual encounter; i.e. '*short time of love*'

T&A [1950s+] soft-core pornography; i.e. '*tits and ass*'

t.b. [1920s+] (Aus.) a pair of large and shapely female breasts; i.e. '*two beauts*'

t.n.t. [1960s+] the female breasts; i.e. '*two nifty tits*'

t.o.s. [1960s+] (US) men picked up in the street; usu. used by hotel clerks in those hotels which let out rooms to working prostitutes; i.e. '*tricks off the street*'

v.w/e [1960s+] used in sex contact ads; i.e. '*very well-endowed*'

w.g.f. [1960s+] *whole girl fantasy*; used by transsexuals

Romance: Knickers Off ...

There is a long-standing tradition of inscribing sentimental acronyms on the envelopes of love letters, particularly those posted by soldiers from abroad ...

b.u.r.m.a. [late 19C+] i.e. '*be undressed/upstairs, ready, my angel*'

e.g.y.p.t. [20C] i.e. '*eager to grab your pretty tits*'

h.o.l.l.a.n.d. [1940s+] i.e. '*here our love lies and never dies*'

i.l.u.v.m. [20C] i.e. '*I love you very much*'

i.t.a.l.y. [1940s] i.e. '*I trust and love you*'

n.o.r.w.i.c.h. [1940s+] (orig. by soldiers) i.e. '*(k)nickers off ready when I come home*'

p.o.l.o. [1990s] i.e. '*pants off, legs open*'

w.a.l.e.s. [1980s] i.e. '*will arrive late, expecting sex*'

To which the addressee might playfully reply:

p.u.m.a. [1990s] '*panties up my arse*'

s.w.a.l.k. [20C] i.e. '*sealed with a loving kiss*'; other versions include s.w.a.k., '*sealed with a kiss*'; s.w.a.n.k., '*sealed with a nice kiss*', and s.w.a.l.c.a.k.w.s., '*sealed with a lick 'cos a kiss won't stick*'

SIMILES, SUNDRY

See also COMPARISONS, MISCELLANEOUS; MONEY; SPEEDY

be behind like a slave-driver [20C] (W.I.) to beg, to harass, to pressurize

bleed like a (stuck) pig [17C+] to bleed heavily, to lose a good deal of blood

built like a brick shithouse [1920s+] (orig. US) describing a very strong, muscled man, or woman, who resembles a squat, four-square, solid edifice, often euphemized as 'schoolhouse', 'outhouse' etc; also (Aus.) **built like a brick dunny**

buzz around like a blue-arsed fly [late 19C+] to be excessively busy, often to the detriment of others, to rush around headlong

come down on someone like a ton of bricks [1910s+] to unleash the full force of one's anger or aggression on someone

come like a parolee at the ho shack [1970s] (US Black) to move very fast

come on like a test pilot [1940s] (US Black/Harlem) to act in a speedy, efficient manner

done like a dinner [mid-19C+] (Aus.) 'done to a turn', i.e. utterly defeated

done up like a kipper [20C] beaten up

drink like a fish [17C+] to drink heavily

feel like a boiled rag/piece of chewed rag/string [20C] to feel ill

feel like a million dollars [1910s+] (orig. US) to feel excellent, very cheerful, extremely well, in the best of spirits, thus **taste like a million**, to taste very good

flat out like a lizard on a log [1940s+] (Aus.) lying flat out on one's face

fuck like a bunny [20C] to copulate enthusiastically

fuck like a stoat [late 19C+] to copulate enthusiastically

get on like a bushfire [1940s] (Aus.) to get on well with someone, to make friends fast

go down like a lead balloon [1950s+] (orig. US) usu. of an idea or suggestion, to find no favour or support whatsoever

go like a wanker's elbow [1990s] to be extremely busy

grin like a street-knocker [mid-19C+] to grin broadly

have eyes like a shithouse rat [1910s+] to have shifty, but acute eyes

laugh like a drain [1940s+] to laugh uproariously

lay out like a carpet [1900s–50s] (US) to knock unconscious

lie like a bastard [1960s+] to tell bare-faced lies

like a baby's arm with an apple/orange in it/like a baby's arm holding an apple/orange [1930s+] used to describe an extra-large penis

like a beer bottle on the Coliseum [1940s+] (Aus.) conspicuous

like a blue-arsed baboon [1950s+] headlong, very fast

like the cocky on the biscuit tin [1980s+] (Aus.) useless, impotent, non-participant; from tins of Arnott's biscuits, which pictured a cockatoo, which was thus 'on' the tin but not 'in' it

like a monkey with a tin tool [mid-19C] impudent, cheeky

like a nun in a knocking shop [late 19C+] utterly incongruous

like a pimple on a cow's/bull's/pig's arse [20C] utterly insignificant

Three Similes of Superfluity

like a baby at a wedding [1930s–40s]

like a pork chop at a Jewish wedding [1930s+]

like a spare prick at a (lesbian) wedding [1960s+]

like the hammers (of hell) [20C] very quickly

like two apples in a bag [1950s+] (orig. US) a ref. to well-formed buttocks, whether on a boy or girl

like two pennorth of tripe [20C] used of something considered useless, worthless, unpleasant

like whelks behind a window-pane [1890s–1910s] said of the eyes of a person who wears very thick glasses

lit up like a Christmas tree [20C] very drunk

look like a monkey fucking a football [1960s+] (US) to look utterly absurd

looks like the devil had an auction [20C] (US) a remark offered when faced with a particularly untidy house

mind like a sink/sewer [1930s+] an imagination that invariably sees a smutty meaning or double-entendre in any statement

need like a hole in the head [1940s+] to not need at all

out like a light [1930s+] collapsing – through a blow, drink, drugs, exhaustion – instantly

out on its own like a country shit-house [1910s+] (N.Z.) unique, unrivalled

run around like a cut cat [1950s] (Aus.) to be very angry

run like a hairy goat (Aus./N.Z.) **1** [1950s+] of a racehorse, to run very badly; occas. to run fast. **2** [1960s+] of a motor vehicle, to run badly

shine like a diamond/dime in a goat's ass [1980s+] (US) to shine very brightly

shine like a shilling up a sweep's arse 1 [1900s–30s] to shine very brightly. **2** [1960s] to be very conspicuous

shoot through like a Bondi tram [1940s+] (Aus.) to leave very quickly, to run off (after *Bondi*, a suburb of Sydney)

smell like a rose [20C] (US) to appear pure and innocent

speak/talk like a book [mid-19C+] to appear well-educated and literate

standing there like a tit in a trance [20C] said of someone who is lost in thought, abstracted

stick out like a sore thumb [1930s+] to be very conspicuous or obvious

sweat like a bull [late 19C+] to perspire profusely

sweat like a nigger (at election) [1900s–50s] **1** (US) to sweat profusely. **2** to work very hard

take off like a big-assed bird/bat out of hell [1940s+] (US) to leave very quickly

talk like a ha'penny book [20C] (Irish) to talk nonsense (from *ha'penny book*, a comic, cheap paperback)

talk like a man with a paper ass [1940s+] (US) to talk nonsense

throw money around like a man with no hands [1940s] (Aus.) to be very mean

up and down like a fiddler's elbow [late 19C+] very restless

Stinking Similes

off like a bucket of prawns in the hot sun [1960s+]
1 stinking, rotten. 2 leaving very quickly

smell like a badger's touch-hole [17C–late 19C] to smell
very unpleasant

smell like a ram-goat [20C] (W.I.) to smell disgusting,
esp. after one has passed out drunk and urinated down
one's legs

smell like a whore's garret [20C] to smell strongly of
cheap perfume, as applicable to a man or a place as to a
woman

up and down like a yo-yo [1930s+] used of one who is unable
to keep still or whose emotions alternate continually between
optimistic and pessimistic

work like a kaffir [1970s+] (S.Afr.) to work very hard

wriggle like a cut snake [20C] 1 (Aus.) to act the toady. 2 to
be evasive

Like a Cow's Cunt: Symilies from Ye Olden Times

all on one side like Lord Thomond's cocks [late 18C–early
19C] said of a group of people who appear to be united but
are, in fact, more likely to quarrel (from the 18C anecdote of
Lord Thomond's (1769–1855) Irish cock-feeder, who foolish-
ly confined a number of his lordship's cocks, due to fight the
next day for a considerable sum, all in the same room.

Stereotyped for the story as a stupid Irishman, he supposedly believed that since they were all 'on the same side', they would not squabble. He was wrong, and the valuable cocks destroyed each other)

blush like a blue dog [late 18C] not to blush at all

die like a hen [18C–19C] (Scot.) to die unmarried

die like a rat [late 17C–late 18C] to be killed with poison

eat like a beggar man and wag one's under jaw [late 18C] 'a jocular reproach to a proud man' (Grose 1785)

fit like a ball of wax [mid–late 19C] of clothes, to fit very tightly

follow like a tantony pig [late 18C] to follow closely (from *anthony/t'antony*, the runt of the litter, St Anthony being the patron saint of swineherds, and always represented as accompanied by a pig)

grin like a basket of chips [late 18C–early 19C] to grin broadly

---

Five Similes of Prominence

standing out like …
– **a shit-house in the fog** (Can.)
– **a sore thumb**
– **chapel hatpegs** (usu. of erect nipples)
– **cod's ballocks**
– **dog's bollocks**

---

hand like a foot [early 18C] clumsy, badly shaped handwriting

have a jaw like a sheep's head [late 19C] to be all talk and no action

have a mouth like a cow's cunt [late 19C] to be very talkative

like a duck on a dough-pile [late 19C] (US) heavily, solidly, thus phr. *landed like a duck...*

like a Durham steer in a ploughed field [late 19C] (US) very clumsily

like a rope-dancer's pole with load at both ends [late 18C–early 19C] used of a very stupid and slow person

like as an apple to an oyster/lobster [mid-16C–late 17C] utterly different

like a snob's cat – all piss and tantrums [early–mid-19C] a general phr. of derision or disdain

long and narrow, like a Welsh mile [late 18C–19C] said of anything that is thus shaped (like a *country mile*, a Welsh mile tended to be longer than its stated measurement)

off like a lamplighter [mid-19C–1910s] leaving very quickly

roar like a town bull [late 18C–mid-19C] to make a good deal of noise

shine like a shitten barn door [late 18C–early 19C] to shine brightly

simper like a frumety-kettle/furmity-kettle [18C–19C] to smile, to look cheerful (SE *frumenty*, a dish made of hulled wheat boiled in milk and seasoned with cinnamon, sugar etc.)

sings more like a whore's bird than a canary bird [late 18C–early 19C] said of one who has a strong, manly voice

sit like a monkey on a gridiron [late 19C–1920s] of a horse-rider, to sit badly on a horse

sit like a toad on a chopping-block [late 18C–late 19C] to sit badly on a horse

sleep like a cow [late 18C] to sleep like a married man, i.e. with one's back to one's wife

smile like a brewer's horse [mid-17C] to look satisfied or pleased with oneself.

sold like a bullock in Smithfield [early–mid-19C] badly cheated (ref. to *Smithfield*, formerly London's meat market)

speak like a mouse in cheese [late 18C–early 19C] to speak quietly or indistinctly

spring like a halfpenny knife [late 19C] floppy, lacking tension or resilience

squint like a bag of nails [late 18C–mid-19C] to squint in a noticeable manner

stare like a dead/stuck pig [late 17C–early 18C] to gape, to stare at fixedly

swear like a cutter [mid-16C–17C] to swear with great vehemence (from *cutter*, a braggart)

swill like a tinker [late 17C–early 19C] to drink to excess

talk like a penny/halfpenny book [late 19C–1900s] used by an illiterate person of one whose fluency is considered suspect and overly 'clever' (from *penny/halfpenny book*, a comic, cheap paperback)

toil like a tar on a horse/horseback [late 18C–early 19C] to work clumsily (alluding to the incongruity of a *tar* (sailor) on a horse)

SLIPS *See also* **FLIES**

Awkward Social Situations No. 11

What to Say to a Woman whose Slip is Showing

charlie's dead [1950s+] (UK juv.)

cotton is low [20C] (US, mainly South)

daddy loves you best [20C] (US)

it's snowing down south [1940s+] (Aus.)

Monday comes before Sunday [1960s+] (US)

Mrs White is out of jail [1960s+] (US)

p.p. [late 19C–1910s] a warning from one girl to another ('*p*etticoat is *p*eeping')

showing next week's washing [20C]

s.s. [late 19C–1910s] a warning from one girl to another ('*s*himmy's *s*howing')

there's a letter in the post office [mid-19C+]

white man's/whitey's out of jail [1960s+] (US)

your boyfriend's thinking of you [20C] (US)

SPEEDY: OFF LIKE A BRIDE'S NIGHTIE

See also SIMILES, SUNDRY

flat out like a lizard drinking [1940s+] (Aus.)

go like a bat out of hell [20C] (orig. US)

go like a bird [1940s+] of an automobile, or any vehicle, to go fast and smoothly with no mechanical problems

go like a bomb [1950s+]

go like a cut cat [1960s+] (N.Z.) to leave or run off at speed

go like a dingbat [1950s+]

go like shit off a shiny shovel [20C] (Aus.)

off like a bride's nightie [20C] (Aus.)

off like a robber's dog [20C] (Aus.)

off like a school boarder's lunch [20C] (Aus.)

off like Grandma's pants on Fathers' Day [20C] (Aus.)

quick as a bumnut through an eggslice [20C] (Aus.)

quick as a rat up a rope/drainpipe [20C] (Aus.)

In contrast, it might be said of a very slow person that …

… he couldn't catch a cold [20C]

Awkward Social Situations No. 12

What to Say to a Person Who is Spouting Unadulterated Hogwash

your ass is sucking wind [1940s+] (orig. US)

or one may say that said orifice is absorbing …

– buttermilk [1950s+] *or*

– blue mud [20C]

Alternatively one may diplomatically enquire whether it is the …

rum talking? [20C] (W.I.)

If this has no effect, then try …

thank you and good night [1970s+]

STUFF AND NONSENSE

See also DISMISSAL AND CONTEMPT; NEGATION,
   ABSOLUTE

all fuss and feathers [late 19C] (US)

all gas and gaiters [late 19C+]

all in the eye [mid–late 19C]

all jemmy! [19C]

all my eye and (my) elbow [late 19C–1900s]

all my eye and my grandmother [late 19C]

all my eye and Tommy [late 19C]

all my whiskers [1930s]

all pills! [late 19C+]

blah, blah, blah [1930s+]

cut the crap! [1930s+]

get off! [1950s+]

go to grass (and eat hay)! [19C+] (US)

horse manure [1920s+] (US)

horse pucky [1970s+] (US)

kiss off! [1930s+]

knickers to you! [1970s+]

pull the chain! [1920s] (US)

tats and all! [early 19C]

you have your porridge [1990s]

All My Eye and Betty Martin

[late 18C+] utter, absolute nonsense (the identity of
Betty Martin continues to be a source of controversy.
The 20C lexicographer Eric Partridge suspected
that she was a late 18C London character and that
no record of her existed other than this catchphrase. Earlier lexicographers – Jon Bee (1823) and
Hotten (1860) – referred to the alleged Latin
prayer, *Ora pro mihi, beate Martine* ('Pray for me
blessed Martin', i.e. St Martin of Tours, the patron
saint of publicans and reformed drunkards). This
prayer has yet to be found in any version of the
liturgy. Writing in 1914, Dr L.A. Waddell suggested
another Latinism, *O mihi Britomartis* ('O bring
help to me, Britomartis'), referring to the tutelary
goddesss of Crete. More likely is the idea, proposed
in Charles Lee's *Memoirs* (1805), that there had
once been 'an abandoned woman called Grace',
who, in the late 18C, married a Mr Martin. She
became notorious as Betty Martin, and 'all my eye'
was apparently among her favourite phrases. A
northern English version of the phr. has Peggy
Martin, while London usages include '… and my
elbow' or '… and my grandmother')

STUPID: A FEW ROOS LOOSE
IN THE TOP PADDOCK

See also DAZED AND CONFUSED; MAD

all up in the koolaid without knowing the flavour [1990s+]
(US campus)

buried in a napkin [19C]

can't walk and chew gum at the same time [1960s+] (US)

couldn't see a hole in a forty-foot ladder [late 19C+]

couldn't find a grand piano in a one-roomed house [20C]
(Aus.)

**couldn't tell the time if the town-hall clock fell on top of
him** [20C] (Aus.)

cruising with one's lights on dim [20C]

Awkward Social Situations No. 13

What to Say when Cornered by a Blithering Idiot

if brains were shit, you wouldn't have enough to fart
[20C] (Aus.)

**if your IQ were 2 points higher it would be the same as
a bloody stone** [20C] (Aus.)

pull a clue out of the clue bag! [1980s+] (US campus)

you don't know whether you want a shit or a haircut [20C]

you haven't got the brains you were born with [20C]

you have an IQ of 2, and it takes 3 to grunt [20C] (Aus.)

dead from the neck up [1910s+]

dumb as four o'clock [20C] (US)

dumber than a box/wagon load of rocks [20C] (Aus.)

fat in the forehead [20C] (Ulster)

free of sense as a frog of feathers [20C] (Aus.)

hasn't enough brains to carry guts to a bear [19C–1900s]

have only fifty cards in one's deck [1920s–40s] (US)

he must have two pricks – he couldn't be that stupid from pulling one [20C] (Aus.)

he would fuck up a wet dream [1960s+]

he wouldn't know a tram was up him till the bell rang [20C] (Aus.)

he wouldn't know if a brass band was up him unless he got the drum [20C] (Aus.)

he wouldn't know if his arse was on fire [20C] (Aus.)

he wouldn't know if someone was up him sideways with an armful of deck chairs [20C] (Aus.)

if brains were dynamite, he wouldn't have enough to blow his nose [20C] (Aus.)

just fallen off the cabbage/turnip truck [1980s] (US)

looks like he wouldn't piss if his pants were on fire [20C]

musclebound between the ears [1910s–40s] (US)

nobody home [20C] (orig. US) used of someone who is dull or stupid; ext. to **the lights are on, but no-one's home**

no more sense than a native bear, an' not half as good-lookin' [20C] (Aus.)

no more wit than a coot [16C]

He Wouldn't Piss if his
Pants Were on Fire

not enough brains to give 'imself a headache [20C] (Aus.)

not enough sense to pour piss out of a boot [20C] (US)

not the sharpest tool in the shed [20C] (Aus.)

on the wrong side of the hedge/door when brains were given out [19C+]

play with 44 cards in the deck [1960s+]

sharp as the corner of a round table [late 19C]

she wouldn't know if someone was up her [1910s+] (Aus.)

sillier than a two-bob watch [20C] (Aus.)

so dumb she thinks her bottom is just to sit on [late 19C+]

soft as shite [late 17C+]

some mothers do have 'em [1920s+]

subtle as a dead pig [late 17C–early 18C]

the lift doesn't reach the top floor [1990s]

they ought to slap a cow's cunt over his head and get a bull to fuck some sense into him [20C] (Aus.)

thick as a doctor's wallet [20C] (Aus.)

thick as poundies [late 19C–1900s] (from Irish *poundies*, potatoes mashed with onion and milk)

thick as two short planks [1950s+]

thicker than two tons of dog shit [20C] (Aus.)

thin in the upper crust [20C] (US)

up against the wall/wire/ropes/the bit [1960s+] (US campus)

wise as Waltham's calf [early 16C–mid-19C] (from the saying *as wise as Waltham's calf that ran nine miles to suck a bull*)

world's only living brain donor [20C] (Aus.)

S'WONDERFUL, S'MARVELLOUS

Miscellaneous Expressions of Approbation and Delight

aces and eights [1920s]

ah seh one [1980s+] (W.I./UK Black teen)

(all) fine and dandy [20C]

all that and then some [1960s+] of a person or object, in
  possession of all good qualities

A-OK [20C]

back of the net! [1980s]

bang-up to the mark (or bang up to dick) [early 19C+]

best/greatest thing since sliced bread [1960s+]

big thing on ice [mid-19C] an amazing thing

cool breeze! [1960s+]

curl-the-mo (also kurl-the-mo, curl-a-mo, kurl-a-mo)
  [1940s+] (Aus.)

done to a turn (also done to a burn) [early 19C+]

far out! (also far away!) [1960s+]

fine as fivepence (also fine as fippence) [late 18C]

fit as a fiddle (also fit as a trivot, fine as a fiddle) [late 16C– early
  17C] ideal, perfect, most opportune (later, 'in good health')

good as wheat [19C]

good biz! [late 19C–1910s]

good deal! [1940s+] (US)

grand as ninepence [mid-19C]

high as nine [mid-19C–1940s] (US)

The Dog's Bollocks

in goat heaven and kiddie kingdom [20C] (W.I.) to be in
absolute bliss

in the groove [20C]

it's a peg [1930s+] (Aus.)

jam-up and jelly-tight (also **jelly-tight**) [1960s+] (US Black)

jolly d! [20C] (juv.) i.e. '*jolly d*elightful'

on the money [1940s+] (orig. US)

out of sight (also **outasight**) [late 19C+]

out of this world (also **out of the world**) [1920s+]

right on! [1950s+] (US Black, but taken up by White hippies,
radicals etc.)

right up one's barrel [1940s+] (Aus.) completely to one's
taste

sex with Jesus! [1980s+] (orig. US)

that beats creation (also **that licks creation**) [early 19C+] (US)

that's the stuff [late 19C+]

that's up against your shirt [late 19C] said of an outstanding
or comprehensive victory or success

to die (for) [1970s+] (US)

to kill for [20C]

to the max [1960s+]

top-hole! [20C]

top of the bill [20C]

up in/to G [late 19C–1920s] (US)

up to the hammer [late 19C]

whacko the diddle-oh [1960s+] (Aus.)

won't quit (also **won't stop**) [1960s+] (orig. US) outstanding; e.g. 'she's got legs that just won't quit'

wouldn't that freeze you? [1930s] (US) isn't that amazing?

wouldn't that rattle your slats? [late 19C+] (US)

you wouldn't read about it! (also **you wouldn't know about it**) [1950s+] (orig. Aus.) a phr. describing anything amazing or unbelievable

Neato Jet!

Enthusiastic endorsements by US teens and students:

cool beans! [1980s+] (US teen)

it's a gas! [1960s+] (US teen)

killer beans! (also **killer boots!**) [1990s+] (US teen)

mouth-o! [1980s+] (US campus) this tastes excellent

neato jet! [1990s+] (US teen)

out of state! [1970s+] (US campus)

stoke me! (also **stoke me up!**) [1980s+] (US campus)

straight from the fridge! [1980s+] (US Black/teen)

the only! [1990s+] (US teen)

The Dog's Bollocks

Excellence involving animals or their by-products:

bang up to the elephant [late 19C–1900s]

eggs in the coffee [1920s–30s] (US)

off the meat rack [20C] (US Black)

that ain't chopped liver [1950s+] (US)

A Slap in the Belly with a Wet Fish

that's the Limburger [late 19C–1900s] *Limburger* is a kind of cheese

the dog's bollocks [1920s+]

the mutt's nuts [1920s+]

this beats cockfighting (also **this beats thunder**) [19C]

whacko the chook (also **whacko the goose**) [1970s+] (Aus.)

whale of a ... [1910s+] e.g. 'that was a whale of a party'

whole hog [early 19C+] (orig. US) absolutely everything, the very best of something; usu. in phr. **go the whole hog**

Just dandy

just like mother makes it [1910s+]

just the hammer (also **that's the hammer**) [mid-19C+]

just the ticket (also **just the job**) [mid-19C+]

just what the doctor ordered [1910s+]

Things Could be Worse

In fact, they are **better than a ...**

– **kick in the ass with a frozen foot** [20C] (Can.)

– **poke in the eye with a blunt/burnt stick** [mid-19C+]

– **slap in the belly with a wet fish** [late 19C+]

– **smack in the eye** [20C]

– **thump on the back with a stone** [18C]

TOASTS

back of the net! [1980s]

both ends of the busk! [late 18C–early 19C] (from *busk*, a corset, its upper end at the breasts, its lower end towards the vagina)

bottoms up! [20C] (orig. RN)

bung ho! [1920s+]

down the hatch! [mid-19C+] (orig. naut.)

happy days! [1910s+]

here goes! [early 19C+]

here's how! [20C]

here's looking at you! [20C]

here's to the skin off your nose [1920s–50s] (orig. naut.)

inside and outside! [early–mid-19C]

may your prick and purse never fail you! [early 18C–mid-19C]

milk and water! [late 18C–early 19C] (the ref. is to the female breasts and vagina which give, respectively, milk and urine)

no daylights or heeltaps! [mid-18C+] i.e. the space left in a glass between the top of the liquor and the rim; such a space is not allowed when drinking bumpers, hence the toast

tight cunts and easy boots! [late 19C–1910s]

to the best cunt in Christendom! [late 17C–early 18C]

up yours! [20C]

TROUBLE, GETTING INTO *See* **DOO-DOO, BEING IN DEEP**

UGLY, BEING

a face like ...

– **a bagful of spanners** [1970s+] used of someone who has a
  craggy, rough-looking face

– **a coastguard station** [1940s+] to have a chilly, 'stony' face

– **a cobbler's thumb** [1970s+]

– **a stripper's clit** [1990s] a derog. description of the face of
  an unattractive woman

– **the back of a bus** [1940s+]

– **the back of a tram** [1930s–40s]

– **the rear end of a cow** [1940s+]

– **the side of a house** [1940s+]

I wouldn't ...

– **be seen/found dead in/with him/her** [1910s+]

A Bagful of Spanners

– **fuck her with a borrowed prick** [20C]
– **like to meet him/her in a dark alley** [20C]
I wouldn't touch it with …
– **a dog's prick** [1960s]

– a pair of tongs [20C]

– a pitchfork [late 19C]

– a red-hot poker [20C] (Aus.)

– a rotten stick [mid-19C]

– a 10-foot (barge) pole [20C]

– yours [late 19C+]

ugly as a mud-fence (stuck with tadpoles) [20C] (US)

Ugly Australians

a face like …

– a burnt thong

– a cat licking shit off a thistle

Awkward Social Situations No. 14

What to Say when Introduced to an Ugly Person in Sydney

what will you do for a face when the monkey wants its arse back?

you look like something the wolves ate and shat over a cliff

you look like you fell out of the ugly tree and hit every branch on the way down

your face looks like a cat's arse

you've got a head like a dropped pie

A Hatful of Arseholes

– a mile of unpaved road
– a mouthful of mashed-up Smarties
– a robber's dog
– a smacked arse
– a smashed crab
– the north end of a southbound cow

a head like …

– a bucket of burnt thongs

– someone tried to put out a campfire with a screwdriver

– the south end of a northbound camel

about as attractive as a box of frogs

as ugly as a …

– bulldog chewing a wasp

– hatful/bucket of arseholes

– mud fence in a rainstorm

– shithouse rat

if I had a dog that looked like him, I'd shave its arse and
make it walk backwards

I've seen better heads in a piss trough

she could scare buzzards off a meat wagon

ugly as a deep-sea racing mullet

UNHAPPY *See* **DEPRESSED**

URINATE, TO

See also EUPHEMISMS

apple and pip [late 19C+] (rhy. sl. *apple and pip* = backslang
sip = piss)

bleed one's turkey/liver [1920s+]

do the gentleman [1920s]

drain …

– **one's lizard** [20C]

Draining one's Radiator

– **one's radiator** [1940s+]
– **the dragon** [1960s+]
– **the main vein** [1980s+] (US campus)
give the Chinaman a music lesson [20C]
go look at the crops [20C]
leak the lizard [1960s+] (Aus./US)
let one's horse out of the stable [1950s–60s]
pay one's water bill [1970s] (US Black)
piss up a storm [1990s] (US) to urinate for a long time
point percy at the porcelain [1960s+]
rip van winkle [20C] (rhy. sl. = 'tinkle')
shake hands with …
– **an old friend** [1960s+]

– **Mr Right** [1960s+]
– **the fellow who stood up when I got married** [1960s+]
– **the unemployed** [1960s+]
– **the wife's best friend** [1960s+]
shake/knock the dew off the lily [1960s+]
shed a tear for Nelson [mid-19C+]
siphon the python [1960s+] (Aus.)
splash one's boots [20C]
strain the potatoes [1960s+] (Aus.)
take a snake's hiss [20C] (Aus.) (rhy. sl. *snake's hiss* = piss)
wring out one's sock [20C]
wring the dew off the branch [20C]

Awkward Social Situations No. 15

What to Say when You are Desperate

After you with the po, Jane [late 19C–1920s]
have one's back teeth afloat [1960s+]
need to piss like a dressmaker [late 19C] (dressmakers working in sweatshops were not permitted to take a break)
take a Chinese singing lesson [1990s+] to urinate following a desperate need

---

USELESS

See also WORTHLESS

The Useless Antipodean

The useless Australian **couldn't …**

– find his arse with both hands even if his fingers were
   flashlights
– get a job on a shithouse cart
– grow a choko vine over a shithouse
– hit the side of a barn with a handful of wheat
– organize a fart in a chilli-eating contest
– organize an orgy in a brothel (also **organize a fuck in a
   brothel with a fist full of fifties**)
– produce a fart in a liquorice factory
– run a bath
– tell his arse from a hole in the ground

Whereas the useless Kiwi **couldn't …**

– fuck a frog trotting
– see the road to the dunny if it had red flags on it
– sell a statue to a pigeon

As Useful As …

– a back pocket on a T-shirt
– a bag full of farts
– a chocolate fireguard/teapot
– a fart in a colander/hurricane

- a handbrake on a Holden
- a nun's cunt
- a one-legged man in an arse-kicking competition
- an ashtray on a motorbike (or water-ski or surf-board)
- an extra prick at a knock-shop wedding
- genital warts on a ribbed condom
- lips on a chicken
- mudflaps on a speedboat
- pockets on a singlet
- springs on a ballerina's shoe
- tits on a bull

A One-Legged Man in an Arse-Kicking Competition

VIOLENT AND UNTIMELY END, TO BRING ABOUT A

See also CRIME AND THE UNDERWORLD; DEPARTING THIS LIFE; HANGED, TO BE

break an egg [1980s+] (US) (from the phr. 'you can't make an omelette without breaking eggs')

deep six [1940s+] (US) (to put someone *six* feet underground)

do for [mid-18C+] (abbr. SE phr. *do* a bad turn *for*)

send to kingdom come [late 18C+] (from *kingdom come*, the after-life)

kiss off [1940s] (US)

put on ice [1930s]

s.o.s. [1990s] (US) *s*mash *o*n *s*ight, i.e. a contract to murder

throw a brick [1950s–60s] (US Black) to kill someone

VOMIT, TO

air one's paunch [1930s–40s] US

boil off the stomach [20C] (US)

call for hughie [1960s+] (UK society)

call earl (also **go to see earl, earl's knocking at the door**) [1960s+] (US)

call the dogs [1990s] (US campus)

chew the cheese [1980s+] (US campus)

chum the fish [1980s+] (US campus)

chuck/flash/flip/heave/lose/throw/toss/woof one's biscuits/cookies [1990s]

do a cat [mid–late 19C]

drive the porcelain bus [1970s+] (US campus) esp. when hugging the circular (i.e. steering-wheel-shaped) lavatory bowl and vomiting therein

feed the fishes/goldfish/kippers [20C] (US) esp. over the side of a ship

flash the hash [late 18C+] (orig. UK underworld)

flay the fox [mid-17C–late 18C]

go (for) the big spit [1950s+] (Aus.)

holler New York [1960s+] (US) (from the supposed similarity between the sound of *York* and that of retching)

jerk the cat [early 17C]

kiss/bow to/hug/make love to/pray to the porcelain god/goddess [1960s+] (US campus)

lose one's doughnuts [1940s+] (US campus)

lose one's lunch [1940s+] (Aus./US)

Parking a Leopard

paint the town red [late 19C+]

park a custard [1970s+] (UK society)

park a leopard [1960s]

perk up [1960s] (Aus.)

play the whale [1960s–70s] (Aus.)

pop one's cake [1920s] (US)

pump ship [late 18C+]

reverse gears [1980s+] (US teen)

ride the buick [1960s+] (US)

shit through one's teeth [late 18C+]

shoot a cat [1980s+] (UK society)

shoot one's mouth off [mid-19C+]

speak/talk on/to the great white telephone [1960s+] (orig. US)

spew one's ring [1960s+]

spill one's breakfast [20C]

split a gut [late 17C]

spread a technicolour rainbow [1970s+] (US campus)

throw a map [1940s+] (Aus.)

throw one's voice [1960s+] (Aus.)

toss a reverse lunch [1970s+] (N.Z.)

toss one's lollies [1980s+] (N.Z.)

toss the tiger [1960s+] (N.Z.)

Uncle Dick/tom and dick [1970s+] (rhy. sl. 'sick')

water buffalo [1980s+] (US campus)

Blow ...

- **chow** [1930s+] (US)
- **chunks** [1930s+]
- **one's cookies** [1930s+]
- **one's doughnuts** [1970s+] (US campus)
- **one's groceries** [1970s+] (US campus)
- **one's lunch** [1950s+] (US)

W

WEATHER (MOSTLY COLD AND WET)

See also COMPARISONS, MISCELLANEOUS; SIMILES, SUNDRY

cold as a polar bear's bum [1950s+] (Aus.) very cold

cold enough to freeze the balls off a billiard table [1950s+] (Aus.) very cold

colder than a witch's tit [1960s+] very cold

colder than Kelsey's nuts [20C] extremely cold

fine day/weather for ducks [19C] said of a wet day

fine morning to catch herrings on Newmarket Heath [mid-17C–mid-18C] said of a wet day

hot as a three-dollar pistol [20C] (US) said of extremely hot weather

hotter than French love [20C] (US) said of extremely hot weather

light drip-drizzle [1940s] (US Black) a light spring shower

Raining...

... **bullock sterks** [20C]

... **cats and dogs** [early 18C+]

... **cats and dogs and pitchforks and shovels** [19C]

... **chicken coops** [19C]

... **darning needles** [19C]

... **pitchforks and nigger babies** [1930s–60s]

... **trams and omnibuses** [1900s–20s]

rain like a cow/bull pissing on a flat rock [1940s+] (US) to rain heavily

rain like a drunken dog [1930s+] (N.Z.) to rain heavily

the devil is beating his wife with a shoulder of mutton [late 18C] said when it is both raining and the sun is shining

two-dog night [1970s+] (Aus.) a very cold night; from an orig. Aborigine term, the ref. is to sleeping between a pair of dogs to keep warm

WITH IT, BEING

all up in the koolaid [1970s+] (US campus/teen) knowing what is going on; aware of the facts; thus *all up in the koolaid without knowing the flavor*, ignorant, unaware

be wake-ups (also **be (full) wake-up**) [1930s+] (Aus./N.Z.)

Things One Must be Up to ...

- **a thing or two** [early 19C]
- **slum** [mid-19C]
- **snuff** [early 19C+]
- **snuff and a pinch above it** [late 18C–early 19C]
- **snuff and twopenny** [late 18C–early 19C]
- **the cackle/gossip/try-on** [late 18C–mid-19C]
- **the dodge** [mid-19C] (US)
- **the stickers** [20C] (US Black)

What the Alert Person is On ...

– **one's job** (also **one's j.o.b.**) [1950s+] (US Black) later [1970s+] **on one's j.**
– **the ball** [1910s+] (orig. US)
– **the button** [20C]
– **the eightball** [1990s+] (US Black)
– **the key-vee** [mid-19C] (i.e. on the *qui-vive*)
– **the spot** [late 19C]
– **the stick** [20C]

Five Places the In Person is In ...

– **it** [mid-19C+] (US)
– **the cart** [late 19C+]
– **the house** [1980s+]
– **the picture** [1940s+]
– **there** [1930s–60s] (orig. US Black)

bright as a button/new pin/dollar [20C]
bright-eyed and bushy-tailed [1950s+]
down as a hammer/trippet/nail [early 19C]
down to dandy [mid–late 19C]
have all one's buttons done up [mid-19C+]

hepped on [20C]

in full jerry [late 19C+]

know beans when the bag is open/untied [mid-19C–1910s]
  (US)

know what time (of day) it is [mid-19C+]

more than seven [late 19C]

not born yesterday [late 19C+]

not come down in yesterday's rain [late 19C+]

not lost for it [1940s+]

seeing the king [late 19C]

tell what's what/what goes [17C+]

Sometimes, however, one can be just …

too far north [mid–late 19C] too clever, too knowing

WORRIED *See* NERVOUS, ANXIOUS, AGITATED

WORTHLESS

See also USELESS

not worth …

– **a bucket of warm spit** [1930s+] (US)

– **a bumper** [1940s+] (Aus.)

– **a cracker** [1950s+] (Aus.)

– **a crumpet** [1940s–60s] (Aus.)

– **a cuntful of cold water** (Aus.)

– **a (two-bob) fart in a bottle** [1970s+] (N.Z.)

– **a fart in a noisemaker/hurricane/breeze/storm/gale**
  [1960s+]
– **a fuck** [20C]
– **a hill/row of beans** [mid-19C+]
– **a jigger** [mid-19C]
– **a light** [20C]
– **a pinch of (cat's) piss** [20C] (Aus.)
– **a pinch of coonshit** [20C] (Can.)
– **a pisshole in the snow** [1960s+]
– **a rap** [early 19C]
– **a roasted fart** [1960s+]
– **a tiger tank** [1970s]
– **a turd** [early 18C+]
– **diddley-shit/diddly-shot/doodly-shit** [1950s+] (US)
– **dogshit** [1960s+]